PRAIRIE
Legacy

Photo by Jim Ballard.

First Printing; July, 2007
Second Printing; October, 2007

Copyright © 2007, Anne D. Bachner
All rights reserved
ISBN: 1-4196-7283-5
ISBN: 978-1-4196-7283-5

Printed by:
BookSurge Publishing
www.booksurge.com
1.866.308.6235

Layout and design by:
Kristin Mitchell Design
608.987.3370

PRAIRIE
Legacy

ANNE D. BACHNER

The Thomas south pasture, now owned by The Nature Conservancy and called the Barneveld Prairie. Photo by author.

A PRAIRIE VIEW
FROM BLUE MOUNDS

"Stopped at the Blue Mounds at Mr. Brigham's. Extensive view from his house over the prairie for 20 miles and more in all directions. Beautiful country.... Throughout the prairie the most splendid variety of flowers are seen rising above the thickly set grass, which has here and there in large and small patches been mowed for hay, presenting a curious checkered appearance on the table beneath us. The prairie flowers are various in hue, the dark purple masonic or mineral flower, the tall bright purple and red feather, the prairie sunflower, the golden rod, the several small and beautifully variegated flowers interspersed amongst the grass, all render the scene indescribably beautiful."

from *The Journal of William R. Smith* August 20, 1837

North face of stone barn. Photo by Cameraworks.

CERTAINLY THE BARN WILL
LAST LONGER IF IT'S ALL STONE.
...SUCH A BARN WOULD BE A
MONUMENT, REQUIRING MORE OF
YOUR LIFE THAN YOU PROBABLY
WOULD WANT TO GIVE IT.

McRaven, *Building With Stone*, p.163

Harold Thomas, 2007. Photo by Harlen Persinger.

ACKNOWLEDGEMENTS

The Thomas and Osborn families have graciously opened their minds and hearts to this project. Harold was overwhelmingly generous in sharing family letters and photos. His wife Amy, and his sister Margarette were also very helpful, as were the children from both families.

Special thanks to Arnold and Gladys Thuli who helped me understand the Amachers' life as cheesemakers in Switzerland.

I am eternally grateful for those who ploughed through my first draft. Thanks to Katherine Martin, Bill and Evelyn James, Claire Holland, Mary North Allen, and Doug Cieslak. More sincere appreciation to my second draft readers, Lisa Bravine, Roland Sardeson, Melva Phillips, and Gert Peterson. To Marnie Jacobson, Sarena Nelson and Diana Petro, my heartfelt thanks for your helpful criticism.

In the initial stages of this project, I enjoyed the company of my late husband, Robert Bachner, who took an enthusiastic part in our many interviews with the Thomas family. At the end I could not have completed the story without encouragement and valuable criticism and assistance from my sister, Valerie Sokol.

I was very pleased to have found a keen professional editor, Jude Clayton, to review the final manuscript. She not only encouraged me in the final stages, but identified problems and helped me work out their solutions, in addition to spotting errors in syntax and mechanics. She and my designer, Kristin Mitchell, turned the Thomas story into a book for all to enjoy.

Raking hay on the Thomas farm.

AUTHOR'S NOTE TO READER

The saga of the Thomas barn, farm, and family is based on stories, personal records, and recollections, as well as newspapers and histories of the time.

For narrative purposes I invented David's trials as a youth with horses and cattle. I also fabricated the hot summer night when David awakens to Lena's importance in his life. As most readers know, real life is truly "stranger than fiction," so there was no reason to invent the major events in the story of the Thomas family, however, I added imaginative dialogue and transitional events to bring the story to life. To make sure that the "truth" of the family experiences was conveyed, I worked closely with the Thomases.

By connecting the stories of four generations of the Thomases, I have learned to love and respect the family and the values they cherish. As with most real-life stories, some things have been left out, while others are so polished with telling and retelling that they approach mythical proportions, and then a few things will forever remain a mystery, as they should in any self-respecting family history.

Thomas Stone Barn, 2005.

PRAIRIE *Legacy*

THE THOMAS FAMILY, THEIR FARM AND STONE BARN

BY ANNE D. BACHNER

■ ■ ■

Part of the proceeds from the sale of this publication
go to the Driftless Area Land Conservancy.

The mission of the Driftless Area Land Conservancy is to protect the
rural landscape and quality of life in southwestern Wisconsin's Driftless Area.
The Conservancy is focused on preserving our unique natural resources and
cultural heritage as a land legacy for future generations. For more information
write or call 338 North Iowa Street, P.O. Box 323, Dodgeville, WI 53533,
608.930.3252, www.driftlesslandtrust.org.

Picnic at Amacher Hollow.

INTRODUCTION TO THE FAMILY

Walter **Thomas** 1827, called 'Ol **Watt** in his later years, was born April 1st, in Cardingshire, Wales. He married **Margaret Kendrick** who was born in 1834. They immigrated to America sometime after Wisconsin became a state in 1848. Eventually they settled in southwestern Wisconsin near what is now a town called Barneveld. Walter believed a stone barn would make them rich when the railroad came through in 1881.

Walter and Margaret had nine children named **Taliesen (Tallie)**, **Price** 1869, **Seth** 1872, **Thomas**, **David Darius** 1861, **Sarah (Sadie)**, **Charlotte (Lottie)**, **Margaret,** and **Arthur** 1875. The young people helped build the barn before they left for the West.

Margaret's sister had married an Evans. Their farm joined the Thomas land on the west and south sides. **John Evans** attended high school with David Thomas in Spring Green. The Evans boys were a great help building the barn. Later two unmarried sisters ran a hat shop in town.

David Thomas went to the University of Wisconsin to become a lawyer. When his father died, David sacrificed his legal profession to return home to save the farm and barn. He married **Lena Amacher** in 1913. Lena was born in Switzerland. Lena's family, especially her sisters, Ida and Helen, and brothers, Pete and Fred, who lived in nearby Amacher Hollow, were an important part of David and Lena's life.

David and Lena had three children named **Margarette Ruth** 1916, **Walter Arthur** 1920, and **David Harold**, who was born in 1922 and was always called **Harold** or **Harry**.

Harold worked on the family farm all his life. He married **Amy Nelson** in 1946. His passions lay in writing and playing music and saving the barn and farm. He first preserved the south pasture through the Nature Conservancy. Then he preserved the remaining acres of the farm and barn through a conservation easement with the Driftless Area Land Conservancy.

Harold and Amy have four children, **Diana Ruth** 1947, **Regina** 1949 (Jeannie), and **Douglas David** 1951, called **Doug**, who was born in 1951, and **Margaret Ruth** 1956 (**Maggie**).

All **Margarette's** children loved the farm, **Evelyn Ruth** 1943, **Janet Ann** 1944, **Beverly Margarette** 1945, **Mavis Rae** 1946, **Phyllis Faye** 1947, **Ramona Gail** 1951, **Shirley Estell** 1953 and **Thomas Rayman** 1955. The children went to the farm after school and any other time they could to work and play. **Tom** and **Doug** were often inseparable.

Doug Thomas continues to live and work on the farm. Doug used the money from the conservation easement to put a new roof on the barn in 2006.

All photos are from the Thomas family files unless specified.

THOMAS AREA MAP

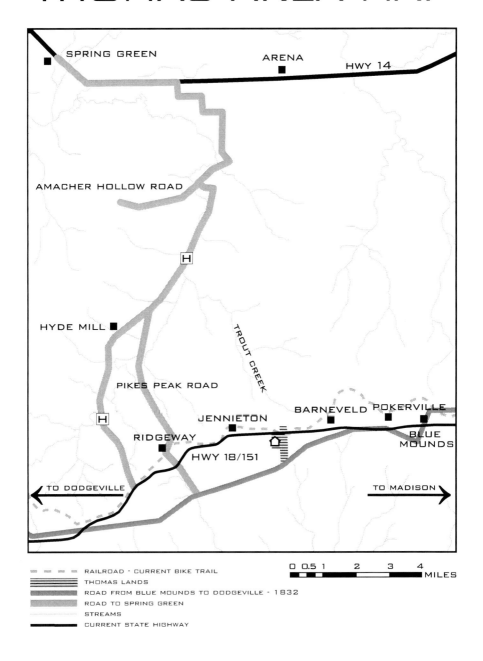

SPRING GREEN

ARENA

HWY 14

AMACHER HOLLOW ROAD

H

HYDE MILL

TROUT CREEK

PIKES PEAK ROAD

H

JENNIETON

BARNEVELD POKERVILLE

RIDGEWAY

BLUE MOUNDS

HWY 18/151

TO DODGEVILLE

TO MADISON

RAILROAD - CURRENT BIKE TRAIL
THOMAS LANDS
ROAD FROM BLUE MOUNDS TO DODGEVILLE - 1832
ROAD TO SPRING GREEN
STREAMS
CURRENT STATE HIGHWAY

0 0.5 1   2   3   4
MILES

Chapter 1

ONE OF THE BOYS

David Thomas was born February 2, 1860, in a cabin near the town of Hyde, Wisconsin, on Pikes Peak Road near Hyde's Mill. (Hyde's Mill as it appears in the 21st century, photo by author).

David began to run down a worn path marked only by his own impatient feet. Here on the prairie the terrain was flat and smooth. Holding his hands out like the wings of a bird, David brushed the grass aside as he rushed along, reveling in freedom from school and anticipation of his father's promise. Encouraged by the wind at his back, he twirled around and raced himself to the first landmark, a stand of trees.

For the moment he had became a fast-moving frigate sailing through an ocean of grass. David had never seen the sea and he had only just read about frigates, but he believed the prairie must be a little like an ocean, especially when the wind was blowing. The dark light of fall and the coolness of the October air urged him on.

The wind changed directions and a restless shadow appeared on the prairie. David looked back and found dark clouds riding the wind's tail, hinting of a storm. Then there was a faint sound that grew deafening. It was a rallying cry of surrender in the face of the coming cold, and a V for victory over the misery of Wisconsin's winter. He stopped completely then, and watched skein after skein of geese flying south.

He remembered now that he was looking for bittersweet. Mother seemed inordinately fond of the brilliant orange bead-like berries. She said they dressed up the cabin. He had arrived at a stand of cedars edging the prairie where he could see the vines showing brightly among the evergreen. They weren't hard to pull down, so he gathered the brightly colored vines and headed home more slowly.

He neared their homestead, set deep in a big stand of oaks. The leaves had finally begun to fall. His progress through them gave him a feeling of power. They snapped and popped delightfully as he strode along looking for squirrels. Then he stumbled on the rough path, strewing bittersweet before him.

As he pulled himself up, brushing off the clinging leaves and bracken and trying to salvage the vines, he considered what his father said the night before. Father had promised David he could ride like the big boys, but it wasn't just learning to ride that he desired, he wanted to leave his mother and sisters to do the housework and work with his father and brothers. He wanted to tell stories of his exploits, like his brothers did, detail by detail, to his family at the dinner table. He yearned for the respect of his older brothers, Taliesen, Price, and Seth. He wanted to be considered an equal to Thomas, just a year older than he was, and he was tired of caring for his sisters, Lottie and Baby Sadie.

He knew that he had been a real help over the summer. Father had let him plant seed corn that spring. His brothers had cut holes in the prairie sod, and he had been the one who dropped seed in the slashes. He was so proud of the corn this year, one would think he had grown it all himself. He was careful not to complain about his endless chores of feeding the pigs and horses, cleaning pens, and hauling wood. His brothers and his father should be able to see he was responsible and ready to ride with them.

Tallie and Seth had given him rides on their horses plenty of times, first in front of them clutching the saddle horn, and then when he got older, behind them bouncing along on the horse's back, holding on for dear life to his brother's belt. Sometimes they had set David on Queenie's broad back with no saddle or bridle and just let her wander around with him clutching her mane for balance.

He was eight years old now, and all he needed was a chance to learn what was necessary to sit in a saddle all day and how to keep a herd of cattle in line. He wanted to ride something besides an old plow horse. Day after day, he would lead Queenie reluctantly to the fence where he would climb on her back. He would hold her mane and kick back. She walked where she wished. At least, when his brothers let him use a bridle, he was able to get her to go wherever he wanted.

He and Thomas had taken the horses on many excursions in the surrounding prairies. To the far east and to the north, great glaciers had gouged out lakes and pushed up hills, but in this area of southwestern Wisconsin, land was undisturbed in what became known as the Driftless Area. The only changes were made by natural erosion.

The boys' favorite adventure was following the creek. They envisioned themselves "discovering" the mighty Wisconsin River, which they knew wasn't too far away. Riding wasn't the same, however, without a saddle. Father promised that tonight would be a good night to ride and really learn some of the skills he needed to go with the boys on the roundup.

The thought spurred him on, and he again ran wildly down the path with little regard for obstacles. Father had said that he needed another rider, and he had looked straight at his youngest boy as he said it. Up until now David had always stayed home when the boys gathered stock. Tonight his father said that he would begin to ride with his own saddle.

Once in sight of the cabin, David stopped, drew his slight frame up as tall as most eight-year-olds going on nine, and walked calmly, almost casually into the cabin where he arranged his offering of bittersweet on the table. Then he ducked out quickly past his mother to the wood pile where he brought in three arm loads of the wood Price had split last night. He avoided making elaborate answers to Mother who invariably asked about school.

"Yes, ma'am, No ma'am," he answered politely, and then moved to the porch where he picked up the slop for the hogs. He wasted no time so that he would be ready when Father gave the word.

He had reason to hurry and get the chores done. The dry, smoky smell of fall was in the air, and the days were getting shorter. David hoped after a few evenings of riding under his father's supervision, that he would be ready to help this year.

Turning his back on the hogs that were pushing forward to get at their share of what looked to David to be a stunningly unattractive mixture of house scraps, he took the long route back to the cabin past the little pasture. At the fence he whistled up Danny, the most beautiful horse they owned and his brothers' favorite.

The horse came at a gallop, stopping just short of the fence. David stroked his dark muzzle thoughtfully and blew softly into his nostrils. Danny shivered, took off with a brief snort and ran to the end of the field, coming back to roll over three times. David watched in admiration. Thirty dollars! Father said that was the way some horse traders valued a horse, ten dollars for each time he went over on a roll. Someday he would dash around on Danny just like Tallie did, with his coattails flying behind him.

"David, dinner's getting cold! You get in here." His mother's call dissolved the picture of himself riding Danny, and he headed slowly back to the cabin. While David had been feeding the hogs and dreaming about riding, guests had arrived for dinner. On their way home from grinding corn at Hyde's Mill, Mother and Father's friends from the old country stopped by. Their wagon was pulled up to the barn, and Father was helping to water and feed the horses.

As his family and friends gathered on benches around the dinner table, David found it hard to be polite when he knew the evening would be devoted to reminiscing about Wales, and not spent on the finer points of horse back riding.

His mother served up a hearty beef stew flavored with the last of the fresh vegetables—squash, carrots, potatoes, rutabagas, and onions from the garden. Behind her, hanging from the ceiling were braids of onions and strings of peppers and dried apples that would have to do for winter meals. She also had made up a kind of corn cake for their dinner which they slathered with newly churned butter, a special treat.

"I've been here over ten years," his father began, as he and Mr. Julian settled around the fireplace to smoke what David feared would be the first of many pipes, "and here we are with a good barn, a snug cabin, over one hundred and fifty head of cattle, and some dang nice horses, not to mention those hogs you sold me last year. Eighteen-seventy was our biggest harvest ever, and if the market holds and the boys can get the cattle to the railhead without them losing much weight, we'll do fine with the stock as well."

"Walter," Mr. Julian nodded, "you've had some mighty fine luck these past years. I envy you all those boys. My passel of girls are mighty pretty, but they aren't much use when it comes to clearing land."

Walter chuckled and tapped his pipe a bit smugly.

David had heard all this before. Everything was better in America, for everyone but him, who would likely be left behind another year at roundup time with Mother and the girls. Baby Sadie was two already. David believed that Lottie, who was going on five, and his mother could handle the house chores without him. He had already been showing Lottie how to pick up wood chips for the fire. She was a girl, but she was a fast learner.

He knew time was running out for horseback riding as his mother finished putting the dishes away and began to light the kerosene lamps. When she finally settled into her rocker to chat with Mrs. Julian, David gave up and headed to the door.

Then, "David, I thought you wanted to ride tonight." His father was pulling on his boots and nodding to Mr. Julian to come along. "Go saddle Queenie," he ordered Price as they headed out to the barn, "We'll see just how good this boy is." The sun was setting, so David knew he wouldn't be on the horse very long, and sadly, Queenie was a far cry from Danny. She was blind in one eye so she tended to list as she moved, and when she moved, it was very slowly, but at least he would be riding.

Price came up with a tattered saddle blanket and smoothed it carefully over Queenie's pathetic sway back. Then, brushing off the bird droppings from a decrepit saddle, he heaved it into place, showing David how to cinch it tightly once, and then again after Queenie let out her breath. David's father gave him a leg up, and after leading Queenie once around the corral, he handed the reins to David and opened the gate.

David straightened in the saddle, tried to settle into the stirrups, which may have been a little long, and imagined himself in the fall roundup. He could see it clearly as he clucked to Queenie and kicked her sides. He would make sure no calves were left behind. He would find the wildest cow and turn back the most errant steer. He kicked back hard, sending the old horse into a brief lope, which ultimately concluded in a slow walk.

Queenie whinnied and pawed the ground. It was only then that David realized she had stopped and was waiting for directions from him. Queenie knew David had left her behind. In her wisdom, she had come full circle around the barn and was waiting patiently beside the water trough. David's father and Mr. Julian were still telling stories and ignoring his demonstration. His brothers were busy in the barn checking saddles and practicing loops with an old lariat. Thomas was cleaning his squirrel gun. No one had seen his inauspicious beginning.

Relieved, David straightened up again, settled in the saddle, tightened the reins, and kicked back in a determined way with both heels. Queenie came to life and started off at what might be called a fast trot, past Father and Mr. Julian. Father began giving him directions, "Stop, go right, back up, trot forward, stop, go left." At first, Queenie balked at David's tentative commands and his clumsy use of the reins.

Then, just as darkness settled over the farmyard, David realized that Queenie was doing what he asked her. That night David learned to communicate with Queenie, and his life as a frontier boy really began.

Chapter 2

THE ROUNDUP

Rounding up the shorthorns.

All the leaves had fallen, and the hills around Hyde's Mill were gray and dismal. Each rain had been colder than the one before. Morning frosts sparkled forecasts of winter's snow cover. "Winter's knocking at our door, boys," Father said, "I do believe we should round up the cattle and ship off the fat steers."

"When do we leave?" Seth asked.

Tallie announced, "I'm asking to ride Danny." Price, as usual, said nothing, knowing that Father always had the last word.

And then Father looked at David and said, "You've been riding for almost two months now, David. We could use your help day after tomorrow."

David just sat and nodded, happier than he had ever been, while his brothers slapped him on the back and then dragged him out to the barn to finish chores. Ordinarily he felt it wise to keep Queenie away from too much exciting activity, but he looked forward to helping push the herd from its summer pasture to the home lot where the animals would be sorted out for sale and slaughter in the stockyards of Chicago.

Most of Walter's cattle were shorthorns. He liked their large size and readiness to fatten. Also, they were quiet on the whole. They were very popular at the public sales and in some cases reached the highest of "fancy" prices.

The next day David went to school, alone, as usual. It was two years since Father had decided that Thomas was old enough to quit school and work with him and the big boys. They were preparing for the roundup by hauling extra feed for the animals they were bringing in. When the hauling was finished, Price went over all the saddles with soap, checking for cracked leathers. Seth practiced with his lariat any chance he had, and Tallie couldn't get enough of the whip, which he cracked at the least provocation, making a general nuisance of himself. Thomas had set up a few stones on the fence and was doing some target practice.

The day of the roundup, kerosene lanterns lit up the frosty landscape while the family hurried through chores. David and Thomas were directed to give the hogs a double ration while the big boys and Father saddled up. Mother packed an inordinate amount of food, what looked like enough for an army on a week's campaign. By the time the sun had brightened the house yard, they were ready to eat breakfast. Mother had set out steaming bowls of oatmeal which they cooled with heavy cream and sweetened with brown sugar. Then she spooned up fried potatoes and ham, advising as she did so to save room for a slab of apple pie. She was taking no chance with them being hungry on the ride.

The children always associated their mother with food—warm,

satisfying, comforting food. She would surprise them occasionally with something special and exceptionally delicious. It might be a little extra sugar on the apple-pan-dowdy or maple syrup for pancakes. They appreciated her efforts, knowing the limitations of her pantry.

The older boys delighted in providing her variety from their hunting and fishing expeditions. It gave them real pleasure to see her usually stern and often sad face brighten into a smile bringing her dark beauty to light. They knew she loved fresh asparagus and silvery trout in the spring. If the conditions were just right, they found morels as well and puffballs in the fall. Those big round mushrooms were sometimes as large as their heads. Mother never failed to prepare a feast after the first deer was shot in early winter. She required all game carefully cleaned, and the boys learned to please her.

Long after she was gone, there was one image of her that they never forgot. She would go to the spring and later the well, with three buckets which she filled to the brim. Carefully setting one on her head, she would pick up the others, one in each hand, and carry them to the house. Her deliberate steps and proud carriage called up exotic images of the circus and foreign lands. All the children practiced carrying three buckets in this way at one time or another and never managed the trick. Mother would laugh when they came home drenched from head to foot carrying two buckets of water, because she knew what they had been attempting.

■ ■ ■

Breakfast over, the boys and men mounted up. On an ordinary day the three-mile drive home from the Spring Green pasture would have been a long day's work. By the time they reached the pasture, Walter and his older boys realized by the ominous sky that this was no ordinary day.

At first David was conscious only of the rumbling in his stomach. It had been many hours since breakfast and it was well past midday. He slid down from Queenie and immediately began collecting wood for a nice big, warm fire to heat tea and warm the meat pies. Father sent the big boys on a slow ride around the pasture to bring up all the cattle. Once the cattle were collected near the gate, the boys would take turns eating quickly. There was much whip-snapping and hollering while David and his father gulped down Mother's lunch. Not once did the older man call attention to the leaden clouds which had settled in the north.

First Seth and then Tallie, then Price and Thomas came to eat. When everyone had finished, the fire was carefully extinguished, and Father made ready to open up the gap fence. By this time the temperature had dropped and the wind had picked up. They could ignore the approaching storm no longer.

As David watched the cows come through the fence, he began to realize the challenge before them. About twenty steers from last year, two big bulls, perhaps twenty cows and an equal number of half-grown calves moved forward following a brown and white natural born leader cow. She had picked up on Seth's saddle bags which he had arranged to "leak" ground corn. The lead cow would follow the corn back home.

According to Father's plan, Seth was in the lead, Father and Thomas rode right flank, and Price and David rode left. Tallie worked back and forth across the rear of the herd, making sure they didn't lose any cattle as they made their way cross-country. The others could hear him whooping and cracking his whip all the way home. Father tried to ignore Tallie's foolishness, but his brothers believed he was acting like a real Western cowboy.

It was easy for David and Queenie at first. "Moove cow," he said as he hurried a hungry cow that had stopped for a few of the remaining shoots of green still visible in what was slowly becoming a wintery landscape. The snow had started with large wet flakes that pulled moisture from the ground and made moving the cattle slow and treacherous.

David rode toward the wayward cow from the right to head her back into the herd. The cow turned abruptly, and fell on one knee in the wet mud, giving Queenie and David a baleful look. Then with a low moo, she staggered up and trotted along with the rest of the herd. Price gave David an approving nod before moving back to keep a couple of calves in line.

As the day wore on, both the cattle and their herders grew tired. David couldn't keep his mind off food. He could see the first helping of stew, and the second, and the warmth of the fire. He brushed the snow from his face and gave a kick to Queenie, "Moove cows, hustle your big old calves, and let's get home." He had enough of riding.

Finally Queenie and the cattle seemed to realize they were headed home, and driving them was no longer a problem. David just held the reins and jogged along with the snow falling quietly around him. He heard only an occasional moo and the soothing swish of large, tired animals moving through the brush. His eyes gradually began to close....

Father awakened him with a pull on his leg announcing, "We're home, David. Good job."

David looked around to see that the cattle had been penned up, and the boys were unsaddling the horses. When they all finally turned toward the cabin, it was long after Mother had lit up the window with a kerosene lamp. Snow continued to fall.

"Sleep riding," Seth teased the next morning. "It must be a new fashion in horse riding!"

David shrugged off the talk about how he had been sleeping in the saddle and had just about fallen off Queenie. He didn't know Father had carried him to bed because he had fallen to sleep again as soon as that stew of Mother's sank thick and warm into his stomach.

■ ■ ■

Next morning, Father silenced Seth with a look and advised the younger boys, "You'll need a good breakfast to help sort the cattle." David grinned at Thomas and devoted himself to his oatmeal. To be needed, to be one of the boys. David was satisfied. Adventures and stories to tell would come later.

As it turned out he did a lot of fence sitting and marking down numbers for Father's records. It was certainly not as exciting as the older boys' jobs which entailed separating the steers for sale and the heifers that would go to market because they were not appropriate for breeding.

Maybe next year, David thought, it would be him moving into the herd and cutting out the half-grown calves and the mama cows Father wanted to save for breeding. Or perhaps Father would let him work one of the gates, opening it for the cows they would keep and closing it quickly so they wouldn't be mixed in again with those they planned to sell. It was lucky for them, and the cattle they were moving, that they didn't get much snow. It stayed cold, and became colder, so the ground was firm. Best of all, the sun came out to bolster their spirits.

From David's position on the fence he still felt part of the scene in front of him. Seth, riding Danny this time, worked like a machine, cutting out the cows and herding them to Price who, alert to his father's decisions, sorted them to sell or keep. Tallie and Thomas maneuvered the gates, leaping quickly in front of them to wave a hat, and then back again to stay clear of the frightened animals. Tallie had the look of a matador as he "played" with the frightened animals. Thomas was particularly good at jumping completely over the fence when necessary.

Then Danny's startled whinny cut the air, and David turned to see Seth half out of his saddle. A panicked heifer had hit Seth's horse broadside, and he had lost a stirrup and his seat in the saddle. David held his breath. Seth was a big boy, and he would grow to be an even bigger man, thick, sturdy, relaxed, and steady. When he rode a horse, they seemed of a piece. The only words Father spoke as they watched Seth shorten the reins, right himself in the saddle, and find his stirrup were, "Steady boy, steady, steady."

It wasn't until they had finished cutting out the cull cows and the one lazy old bull Father had decided to sell, that David realized he wasn't going with his father the next day. The cousins from nearby Jennieton were to arrive next morning to help move the cattle to the railroad in Arena. David was to stay at home with Mother and the girls again.

That night at dinner David ate some of Mother's chicken and dumplings, but they didn't taste quite right. He watched resentfully as his Mother tended to Sadie, who was fussy and cutting her back teeth. Trying not to disturb them, he slipped from the bench, dragged on his heavy jacket and left the cabin. Ignoring Lottie who always wanted to follow him, and the calves who were bawling noisily as they searched for their mothers, he headed for the barn. He found Price cleaning his deer rifle. Never one to say much, Price seemed to understand David's disappointment. As he clicked the rifle barrel closed, Price suggested David might like to go with him the next time he went deer hunting.

The next morning Tallie beat David around the shoulders, moaning and complaining that they wouldn't be able to keep the cattle in line without his help. Thomas gave a kind of superior smile every time he caught David's eye. Father kept checking the sky where clouds were gathering once again. When the cousins arrived, Father was ready to ride off as soon as Mother had filled the saddle bags with food. He was determined to get the cattle to Arena before the storm hit. David turned his back as they rode away.

Chapter 3

THE FIRST FIRE

East end of stone barn long after the events in this chapter.
Photo by Jim Ballard.

The day had been long and dreary without his brothers. By the time he finished chores, it was almost dark and the wind had come up, blowing around everything not nailed down. David burst in the cabin door, shutting it tightly behind him. Though Mother's leftover warm stew smelled good, he still wished he were eating cold pasty and beans before bedding down with the boys and the cattle. It didn't seem fair to be home with the girls again.

"Try this bread pudding and treacle," Mother said, hoping to sweeten his mood. It was David's favorite, and he gave his mother a small smile as he allowed the pudding and thick sweet syrup to slide down his throat.

The wind reflected David's rebellious feelings and kept him awake for awhile, tugging at the shingles and knocking on the panes of glass in their window. It seemed as if he had just settled into sleep when he awakened to hear Sadie crying. Lottie kept repeating, "Mother, Mother, Ma, Ma." The wind was screeching and whistling through the cracks in the walls so loudly that it was hard to be sure he wasn't dreaming.

Then Mother was fairly slapping him, "Get up, get up," she said and it wasn't morning. It was still night, and the moon was obscured by dark clouds. Then David saw the flames.

The roof was on fire just above the fireplace. It was a small area, just enough to light up the cabin. As he watched, the light became brighter and brighter.

Mother was moving like a fury, loading clothes and books into quilts which she tied at the corners. As soon as she saw David was awake, she began hollering orders. "Get dressed now! Wrap Sadie in a quilt and put her in the barn. Then come back for a load." "Lottie," she ordered sternly, "you go with David and take care of Sadie." Lottie clung to David relentlessly and continued to cry in hysterical hiccups all the way to the barn. Once there, he dug a hollow in the hay and he settled her and Baby Sadie into it, she didn't want him to go.

"Wait here for Mother, you have to be a big girl now," he told her sternly. He must have spoken louder and more directly than he was accustomed because she paused in her grief to look at him with wide eyes. He nodded to her, hugged both the girls and headed quickly back to the cabin, leaving them to comfort each other.

From the outside he could see what Mother knew. They had only minutes before the roof would fall in and their cozy home would burn to ashes in the wind. He paused in the open doorway. His mother shoved a lumpy bundle into his hands. She had collected the Bible, a family album, and her patchwork basket for him to carry out. Then she turned to lift Grandma's parlor rocker into her arms.

David looked back at his mother after he left the cabin. Hair streaming, face red with the heat and frustration, her arms laden with her single family heirloom, his mother's image was distorted almost beyond recognition by the fire which was consuming what had once been their comfortable cabin. They both moved quickly away from the inferno.

Once clear of the heat, David found that his mother had already brought out the cradle and her spice cupboard. Then "crackkk," and Mother collapsed into the rocker as they both watched the roof of their home fall in and light up the window with flames. Mother reached for David, and he curled up like a baby rabbit in her lap. Both of them found they couldn't look away. Their eyes were focused on the fire's progress with a morbid fascination. The wind kept teasing the flames as they watched the door fall in and the window panes break in the heat. They heard a roar as the beds and mattresses went up. Finally the walls caught and began to burn. Luckily, the wind was blowing the fire away from the barn.

The heat of the fire finally died down and the cold closed in. It became quiet, and they could hear Sadie and Lottie sobbing. David and his mother turned their backs on the glowing embers and slowly lugged their parcels to the barn. The girls' eyes were red and their little faces were all puffy with so much grief. David and his mother calmed themselves by soothing Lottie and Sadie. Once their bodies were warm, they all relaxed and slept, the four of them, tangled together in their nest of fragrant hay and familiar quilts. The cold night was only broken occasionally by a cry or a muffled sob.

■ ■ ■

David awoke in the morning and felt different in a way that he couldn't understand. For some reason, he felt older. The morning was very still and frigid as he took a walk outside the barn. He couldn't help looking at the sooty site of their cabin, but his fear had disappeared. He knew Mother had needed him, and he had made her proud. All of them were safe, and that made David happy, though he was still boy enough to realize that he was very hungry.

He found Mother and Lottie awake when he returned to the barn. Mother pushed Sadie toward David as she pulled herself erect. She smiled at David and smoothed his tousled hair. "We're going to the Evanses'," she announced quietly so as not to awaken Sadie. Mother's sister's family lived a few miles away near Jennieton.

They had a plan now, and Mother was pleased to have saved her youngest children as well as most of her precious belongings and keepsakes from the old country. However, as she moved quickly to hitch the horses to their wagon, she studiously kept her back to the blackened site of their home. She even walked backward once just so she did not have to look.

The ride through Jennieton to the Evans' family home was slow and quiet. Sadie sucked her thumb, even though she was much too old for that. Lottie clung to Mother's arm and finally slept. Mother let David drive the horses, and she just sat beside him rubbing her hands in the cold. One look at their sad wagon load told of disaster as they pulled into the Evanses' farm. It didn't take very long to empty the wagon and tell the whole story.

Father, Seth, Tallie, Thomas, and Price as well as the Evans boys arrived soon after. Mother couldn't look at Father. "Chimney fire," was all she said and turned away. After they had settled in with the Evans family, Mother refused to talk about what was burned, although she let Father and the boys search through the pyre for her iron skillet and other things that might have survived and would be of use in her new home.

Mother didn't talk a lot after the fire, but when she did, it was about her new home. She wanted a clapboard one, not just logs this time, and she talked about David. She told the story of how he rescued his sister and how she could not have managed without him. David blushed when he heard her going on, but it made him feel almost grown-up.

Winter settled in, and David realized they would be living with Mother's sister and her family until spring. The eleven Evans cousins were fun, but there was not a lot of spare room. The boys slept in the barn most nights, though when it was really cold, they spread their quilts on the cabin floor in front of the fireplace.

In all the excitement of moving and rebuilding, David was still sent to school along with the rest of the younger Evans children. Cousin John Evans was David's age, and he seemed to actually like school, but David found it difficult to sit inside listening to geography and history lessons. The benches were hard, the room cold and unkempt, and the teacher was a girl only a few years his senior. He copied his lessons in perfect script, but could not recall what he had written.

Eventually, David learned to copy and daydream at the same time. He would set his hand to copying and let his mind wander to the cabin they planned to build south of Jennieton. Father had told them the property there had the best hay ground in the United States of America. David was excited. Maybe he would be big enough to do more field work next summer. Jennieton was not too far from Blue Mounds, a huge bulk of earth and stone often covered by a gray haze and haunted by Indians. Perhaps he could ride Queenie up there one day. Perhaps he wouldn't have to go to school.

The unexpected quiet of the schoolroom aroused David. His fingers were wet and sticky with ink, and his copybook had a blot that went through to the next page. He looked up at the teacher's unforgiving face. The next recess David recopied his lesson, read over what he had written, and recited a summary for the teacher. He was convinced that life was exceptionally unfair.

Finally, school let out for winter break. After the flurry of holiday activities, the family settled into a routine of chores, hunting, games, and reading or storytelling by the fire.

Father had become very excited about the future. It was as if the fire and the proposed move had freed him from the past, and he spent most of the long winter evenings poring over copies of *The American Agriculturalist* and a book called *Palliser's Model Homes*. The last might have encouraged Mother, but Father was not looking at the houses. "To the farmer it is one of the most important things how he should house his stock...." He was looking at barns, only barns.

He read aloud, "If you own a farm, and intend to be a good farmer, start out with a determination to have only suitable farm buildings, such as will look well from your neighbor's house." He envisioned building something very special, and it was not a clapboard house.

David and his brothers, with the exception of Price, could not help getting caught up by his father's enthusiasm, but one evening they were especially aware of his Mother's silence. She held her lips firmly together, rocking determinedly as she knitted, and she looked a little as if she had been crying. David had never seen his mother cry, though the family could always tell if she was upset because her face would get still and closed and her dark eyebrows would seem to bristle. When this happened, Father who never let another's feelings interfere with his plans, would always dismiss it by saying, "Mother has her war paint on."

That winter Father and the boys felled logs, and in the early spring they put up a cabin on their new land. Mother moved in somewhat reluctantly. It was a relief for them all to have a home of their own again, but she had hoped for something better than another log cabin.

Chapter 4

MORE SMOKE, 1872

*Statue of Black Hawk outside the Hauberg Museum at the
Black Hawk Historic Site near Rock Island, Illinois.*

Most every year in the early fall the settlers would see smoke from fires burning in the distance. Father and the boys talked about "backfires" and plowing in front of the fire, but it was not until years later that they needed to light one of those "backfires." Mostly they just muttered about the Indians who liked to do a burn in the early spring and fall before their big hunts.

Blue Mounds was the focus of Indian activity and lore. It could be seen for miles around, rising up out of the prairie, and from its summit, one could see in all directions. The Indians called it Old Smoky for the bluish haze that covered it most days. Father explained the haze by saying, "The Winnebagos believed that Manitou, a kind of Indian god, sat beside the spring at the top and smoked his pipe, causing its smoke to cover the Mounds."

David's ears perked up when he heard grown folks mention Indians. They were a popular topic at the mill and at the store. Folks told some whoppers about the old days of massacres and kidnappings. And then there were the stories of the Black Hawk War that erupted in southwestern Wisconsin and finally ended decisively in a swamp near the Pecatonica River. Colonel Henry Dodge and twenty men charged a Kickapoo war party and killed everyone. The encounter was called the Battle of the Bloody Pond.

David couldn't help admire the noble Black Hawk, who pleaded for his people in Washington, and always denied that any of his warriors killed defenseless women and children as the whites did.

In David's youth most folks felt the Indians were a nuisance. They said Indians drank too much, got into fights, and were often "sticky fingered," a nice way of saying they were thieves. Before the end of the Black Hawk War, Indians commonly ransacked settlers' homes when the menfolk were away, scattering frightened women to their neighbors. The Indians helped themselves to whatever articles of food and clothes they could carry.

Perhaps the biggest indictment the Indians suffered was that they were lazy. When David came to his mother and father with these tales, they reminded him that lots of white folks were lazy and foolish as well.

Their comments did not deter David's interest in the exotic Indians. In fact, the more folks talked about how "no count" the Indians were, the more he wanted to see them.

One late spring day the Thomas family awoke to the smell of campfires not too far away. Sure enough, up near their woods was a small encampment of Indians. That afternoon Father did not have to ask David twice to accompany him on a visit.

David could not stop looking at the unusual activity in their woods. There were maybe half a dozen teepees and as many campfires. The Indians themselves were preoccupied but polite as the boy and his father came into the makeshift village. Father paused before one of the teepees and pantomimed smoking to a little boy who was standing around. "Light up," Father said loudly and puffed on his pipe, signaling the little fellow to give him a light. The boy came forward quickly, nodding and taking the pipe from Father.

Father believed that he would get his pipe lit. David admired his father's confidence with the Indians. Father had never disclosed any personal experiences with them, but he treated them like ordinary people, with respect.

David and his father waited for what seemed a long time for a pipe to be lit. Finally, Father pulled back the tent flap to look for the Indian boy. There he was, as Father said, "Like a good fellow, smoking away as if the pipe were his own." Never one to show anger, Father beckoned to the boy. He came forward willingly and silently handed Walter his pipe. The boy was not much older than David, and he made smoking look very satisfying.

The only Indians David had seen before were in a Medicine Show at the feed mill in Hyde where he and his brothers had come with a load of corn to be ground for feed. These Indian folk here in their woods seemed more businesslike and friendly than the scruffy Indians who paraded with the Medicine Show.

David and his father continued their walk through the village exchanging terse, but respectful greetings. At some signal, indiscernible to David and his father, the men gathered in front of the largest teepee, motioning Father to join their powwow. David watched as the men smoked and then finally smiled at a boy his age who was hanging around the circle of men.

When the pipe came to him, Father took a long pull and solemnly passed the pipe to David whispering, "Smoke it, David, or they'll think you don't like them." Never one to disobey his father, David dutifully pulled some of the acrid smoke into his lungs and quickly passed the pipe to the Indian on his left. Then he half-smothered a coughing gasp while Father pounded him on the back and suggested he go home early. David did not waste time loitering around the Indian camp that day, and it was a long time before he ever tried to smoke again.

Father told David later at home that this tribe was on its way to dig ginseng at the Mound. "Sang is magical for them," Father said. "They use it for their medicines and ceremonies. They are in awe of the Mound and its mysterious power," he added. Father respected the Indians, but he wanted to make sure they passed the farm by without "borrowing" too much from the barns and sheds.

■ ■ ■

Sure enough, the Indians visited the Thomas farm the next day, but they acted more like they were on a holiday than out to rob folks. Father made sure the older men all had a plug of tobacco, and Mother passed out dried fruit to the ladies and children.

Sometime after midday the Indian boys began to show a great interest in the pigs. They hung on the fence talking among themselves excitedly with many hand motions. It soon was apparent that they intended to ride the pigs! The pigs were most surprised by their attempts, and the Thomas family never forgot the experience.

David watched carefully. The Indian boys worked in groups of three. Two boys advanced on the biggest pig, one on each side. They synchronized their movements so they reached the pig at the same time, grabbing the front legs which they pulled out as far as they could, completely immobilizing the bewildered animal. Then, the third "little brave" vaulted onto the pig's back and enjoyed his brief ride, whooping and hollering as if he were riding a grizzly. Most of the boys were covered with dirt and manure, but that didn't dim their smiles or diminish their pleasure.

As the Indians finally drifted away in the late afternoon, Father, Mother, and the boys checked their tools and supplies. They were happy to find nothing had been touched. David studied the pigs calculatingly, but decided he was too big to try riding one.

Chapter 5

GOING TO SCHOOL, 1874

One of the Evans boys and his colt.

The years passed, and while David's brothers were busy farming, he was still going to school. The older boys spent the little free time they had grooming Danny, talking horse racing and the West, always the West. Seth and Tallie no longer teased David, instead they turned their attentions to Price, who had become interested in a young lady. Their attacks were unmerciful. "Flossie's coming, better wash your face. She only likes those pretty town boys." Price would blush and clamp his mouth shut, fearful that Father would put a stop to him sparking his girl if he got into it with his brothers.

Father farmed with a passion and was preoccupied with politics and any evidence of progress he found in the newspapers. Mother occupied herself with sewing for Lottie and Sadie's trousseaus. There seemed no end to the clothes and linens that needed decorative edging or embroidery. David himself was almost as big as the teachers at Jennieton and believed himself to be twice as smart.

School had eventually become a pleasure for David. He finished elementary school knowing the first ten chapters of *Community and Citizens* and could recite *Snowbound* with enthusiasm, as well as the more exciting parts of *Evangeline*. Most importantly, it gave him great satisfaction to know the answers to any questions the teacher might pose. He had finally realized that his mother and father just expected him to keep on going to school. In fact, when he finished high school, they took it for granted that he would go to the university in Madison.

The closest high school was in Spring Green, so it seemed natural for David and his cousin, John Evans, to live there during the week and attend school. David was the only Thomas boy sent to high school. It made him feel set apart and special, but he sometimes became lonesome during the week. Often he felt left out of his family's activities and Father's newest obsession with the railroad. His father was convinced that the coming of a railroad to Jennieton would be an economic opportunity for the family.

At first the most challenging part of high school was getting there and back on the weekends. The distance from the family home near Jennieton and Spring Green was almost twenty miles on dirt roads, a long way to walk. So, when David and his cousin heard a grain wagon was going in the right direction, they hitched a ride.

Both boys stayed with the Lloyd Jones family. David found the Jones family very different from his, despite their common Welsh heritage. The boys were taught by the unmarried Jones sisters who everyone called Aunt Jennie and Aunt Nell. Each morning, Monday through Friday, David and John would hitch up the buggy and drive the ladies to the high school in town.

At first, David was frightened of Aunt Nell. She had recently recovered from smallpox and looked frightful. She was very pale and her young face was full of tiny dimples left by smallpox. Aunt Nell was stern in the classroom, but back home on the farm she didn't disguise her unhappiness. Eventually, David's fear gave way to a desire to please her, and he prepared his lessons very carefully.

His mother told him that Nell had been engaged to a good-looking young man before she was taken ill. The suitor came to visit once the danger of catching the smallpox was over. Mother finished the story by adding, "And he never came back." Of course, David recognized gossip when he heard it, but he could not help but believe the story was at least partly true.

After Aunt Nell and her sister Jenny taught the Jones children, John Evans, David, and just about all the smart boys and girls around Spring Green at the time, Aunt Nell went on to River Falls State Normal School in Wisconsin where she became the head of the history department. Perhaps a Normal school cared more about good teaching than about good looks.

Eventually, Aunt Jenny went to St. Paul, Minnesota, where she became director of kindergarten training schools. Though he cared for Aunt Nell, Aunt Jenny was David's favorite teacher. He enjoyed hearing her tales of the Jones family in Wales. She loved an audience and would wait with a patient smile for quiet, and then she would begin.

David related her stories to his mother on his weekends home. She would laugh. "Jenny's a good storyteller," she said. "I can tell some stories that make life in the old country sound frightfully difficult and sad." David's mother did not always agree with the Jones sisters, but she was surely interested in them.

David himself was at first put off by what most folks called their "airs," but it wasn't long before he realized that they weren't putting on airs, they just knew a lot, read a lot, and expected him to read well, figure accurately, and write clearly expressed essays. They taught him to study, but as a boarder, he was also expected to help with chores as well. So, just as if he were at home, David chopped wood, slopped hogs, and mucked out the horse stalls.

When the weather cooperated, the sisters would leave the classroom and walk the nearby prairies where their students learned to identify snakeroot, cupflower, compass plant, and other hardy prairie flowers.

After a few years with this kind of education, David was not only ahead of the class, he was ready to move on. The sisters arranged for him to take an examination for his diploma, which would enable him to teach. The prospect of teaching was daunting to David. He was seventeen years old and simply could not imagine himself as a teacher in a classroom.

He didn't like to think of the prospect, so he hesitantly asked Aunt Jennie about lawyering. He was relieved when she did not protest. She just nodded, smiled that wonderfully encouraging smile, and sat down to write him a note of introduction to a lawyer friend of hers who lived in nearby Spring Green.

Her friend kindly accorded young David the respect due to a prospective lawyer. Welcoming the boy into his back parlor, he motioned him to sit, and without giving him an opportunity to refuse, handed him a glass of sherry. Sitting across from him, the lawyer launched into a complicated monologue on state politics. David, bemused, found himself sipping the sherry and occasionally nodding his head. It seemed natural for him to join the lawyer's family for dinner.

On the way to the dining room, the lawyer and David stepped into the front parlor which served as his host's office. The lawyer pointed to the wall where a framed diploma from the University of Wisconsin hung. "Samuel D. Williams, Bachelor of Laws," it said. David nodded vigorously and said, "I'm a bachelor all right, but I need a lot of tuition money to add 'Laws' to my name." Ever since that visit, he dreamed of being a lawyer, maybe even a judge.

After their father died in 1885, the Jones sisters returned home to begin a boarding school they called Hillside Home School. Their famous nephew, Frank Lloyd Wright, came up from Chicago to build the home building for the boarders. Years before, when David and John Evans had boarded with the sisters' family and gone to high school, neither boy realized he was getting an unusually fine education.

FATHER DREAMS AND DAVID TEACHES IN POKERVILLE, 1877

Stacking hay with David above and Harold below.

There was no question in David's mind. He did not intend to farm. If he could not be a lawyer because of lack of funds, he would head west to the gold country and find wealth and fame there. Other forward thinking fellows felt the same. *The Dodgeville Chronicle* of February 21, 1879 summed up the feelings of David and his brothers, "There is no denying that there is a strong prejudice among young men against farming. Young men raised on the farm look forward with bright anticipation to the time when they shall leave the farm and go to the city to live."

The Thomas boys could not just take off, however. They each needed a stake, and they also had to reckon with their father, who was never content just farming. Walter Thomas had big designs for the future, and he pulled the entire family right into helping him realize his dreams.

David had easily passed the teacher's examination in the early spring of '77, so the best he could do was work for his father at home over the summer and apply for employment in the fall. No one complained about him being home, for the farm was fairly vibrating with activity and a kind of suppressed excitement. Father was at the center of this all, working long days with the cattle and with the men in the fields, and then spending the evenings reading every newspaper he could find. He would even pass some afternoons in town with other men who believed in progress.

"Ol' Watt" they called him behind his back, but it was a title laced with respect for his knowledge and powerful ideas. Father had become convinced that the coming railroad was going to make him a wealthy, successful farmer. He only needed to build an almighty barn to make his plans work. When Mother furrowed her brow, he would read from his favorite publication, *Palliser's Model Homes*, quoting the text about "suitable farm buildings" as if it were from the *Bible*.

It was Aunt Annie's wedding that provided Father the means to realize his dream of a barn big enough to meet the needs of almost 200 head of cattle. Aunt Annie Williams had become a widow when David was too young to notice, but she had endeared herself to the entire family with her cheerful disposition and her delicious apple pies.

Luckily for Father, a man named Isaac Jones also liked apple pies, for after burying his first wife in Waukesha, Isaac moved to Ridgeway where he met and married David's Aunt Annie. The best part for Father was that Isaac was "a very skilled masoner."

The summer after Isaac and Annie's wedding, Isaac and Walter spent an unusual amount of time drawing and figuring. When it came to dimensions, they would lower their voices. "I'm thinking one hundred by forty feet would do it," Walter suggested.

Isaac swallowed hard and looked at his brother-in-law, "You're thinking mighty big, something like a church in size," he said.

David was sure that he heard forty by one hundred feet mentioned at least twice. They were talking about a very big barn. The men would take their pipes to the barnyard after Sunday dinner. Father was unusually active during these discussions, waving his arms as if constructing an air castle. Uncle Isaac stood to one side smoking and nodding his head once in awhile, for he had dreams as well.

At one time David heard them arguing about doors.

"We'll orient her so the back faces the south. Then with a few doors on the back side, we can open up the barn to sun and fresh air," Isaac explained cautiously.

Walter asked, "What do you mean by 'a few'?"

Isaac hesitated before he answered, "Ten."

"Foolishness," Walter insisted. "This barn has no place for foolishness. It's a place of business." They returned to the topic time and again. No matter that Father didn't believe his horses needed a lot of doors, Isaac insisted that the back of the barn exposed to the south was to have ten doors. Isaac recollected a barn in Wales with ten arched doors that could open to the sun's rays. He also wanted Father to consider half or "Dutch" doors with a transom at the top to let in air and even more sunshine.

"Besides," Isaac declared, "the more openings we have, the less stone you have to cut and haul." Finally, Father ceased kicking about the idea, and after the ten "Dutch" doors were built with transoms, one would have thought they were his design.

Mother liked Uncle Isaac because he was such a faithful and consistent Christian and a devoted member of The Welsh Congregational Church and because he never failed to treat her respectfully, elaborately complementing her on her cooking. Even though he and Father were not talking about building a clapboard house, she was glad to have Isaac around.

That same summer Father decided to move their house close to the proposed building site. Mother had believed that her next house would be somewhat better than the current log cabin. A new view out the window of the house she already lived in was not what she had in mind, and she was seriously taken aback by the news. Mother was very pregnant, and she had just about slowed down to a crawl. Perhaps Father felt a little bad about it as well, for he arranged for her to stay a spell with the Evanses while the rest of the family packed up the household, and with some help, almost literally, rolled the cabin down hill.

Sharing work was common in those days so the neighbors came, including the Evans boys, of course, and the men jacked up the house and moved it on rollers onto the biggest hay wagon they could find. It did hang over, but they used two teams of horses. It was downhill only a couple of miles to where Father settled the house. He supervised the construction of a plank floor, and set the boys to digging a new well to which he added a winch.

Mother's last girl was born at the Evans' homestead. The cousins saw this as some kind of family triumph. They really seemed to enjoy petting and admiring comely Baby Margaret and feeding Mother back to her health. When Mother returned home, she admitted that she appreciated the convenience of the new well and winch. However, she neither recovered from Margaret's birth as quickly as she had from her other births, nor did she say much about the house being moved. She did not seem too interested in Father's barn project, either.

Father also planted an apple orchard that year, taking the time to dig the holes carefully for each little twig-like tree. Over the years he would fertilize and prune them himself, ultimately taking great pride in the apples they produced and the wine he made from them.

■ ■ ■

"The stone building will have strength as well as beauty. It's never a good design to have tall, thin columns supporting the roof. Stone demands a visual mass." Father was quoting from one of the many articles he had read.

Isaac nodded, "We'll be making the walls bigger on the bottom and smaller at the top for stability."

Walter and Isaac had planned a symmetrical style that would depend on effective construction techniques and structural detail. There were to be no supporting pillars within the barn. Massive nine by nine-inch by forty-foot beams would make up six bays with the rafters tied vertically into iron bars.

The north-facing facade would be the most impressive. Walter imagined two drive-through entries measuring ten feet in width and eleven and a half feet at the highest point. To anyone who would listen, Walter explained, "A team pulling a loaded hay wagon will be able to pull in one door and go out the other."

And then Isaac described the dramatic arch he would build over each entrance. "We'll need a large protruding keystone measuring eight-by-six-by-twelve inches. It will take nine twelve-by-eight inch cut stones on each side to complete the span and support the wall above." He reviewed his calculations with relish, occasionally drawing out the pattern on a scrap of paper or in the dust. Like the arches he had worked on in Crickhowell, Wales, he would use very little mortar.

Father and Isaac agreed on ventilators for the hay mow, but how many and how large should they be? Even slightly damp hay could heat to the smoldering point and burst into flames. They needed air circulation in such an airtight enclosure. Finally they agreed on seven four-by-six foot ventilators and later added two small doors on the upper south side. Isaac decided to build the doors differently than the ventilators. "We'll make them steeply arched with a keystone and six stones on each side," Isaac decided.

Walter reminded him, "Don't forget, the horses will be down below."

Isaac kept nodding, "And think how light and airy the lower barn would be with all those 'Dutch' doors." There would be more arches as well. Isaac visualized a cathedral/barn that would rival the church he had worked on in the old country.

Born in Crickhowell, South Wales, in 1817, Isaac had immigrated to Wisconsin in 1850 and settled in Waukesha. By the time he and David's father put their heads together, he was in his middle sixties. Certainly he was feeling the effects of carting and laying up stone all his life. Isaac might have been at the peak of his career, or a little on the back side, but one thing was for sure, he had never built anything like what they were planning, except for the church back in Wales.

Walter's boys were aware he wanted to build a very big stone barn. Typical of the patriarchs of the day, Walter saw no need to discuss the details of his plans with his sons. He expected them to help with the barn just as he expected them to help with the farming. However, Walter's plan was not just for himself. He believed that he was building the barn as a legacy for his sons and his grandsons as well.

All that winter Father read and planned. The Methodists in Mineral Point had built their new white sandstone church for $32,000. He was sure that he and Isaac could build a barn for much less. He continued to send away for magazines, and he bought every newspaper available, hoping to learn how to be successful in his new venture.

The railroad was scheduled to be completed in '81, and the barn would be done by then, just in time to make them all rich. He felt that he had the key to success. The barn would store three hundred tons of hay, so he could feed the cows over the winter. Quality cattle were getting between three dollars and five dollars per hundred weight. He could furnish beef to the hungry stockyards in Chicago almost year-round and bank a tidy profit.

However, Father was not just interested in shipping cattle to market, he also raised hogs. The Jennieton newspaper ran an article in January 1879 about his hog business, "WT, our boss hog raiser, sold a very fine lot of hogs the past few days to Mr. Ben Williams in Arena. They were sixty-eight in number and supposed to average three hundred and eighty pounds." Father claimed the average was closer to four hundred pounds, but he liked the appellation, "boss hog raiser."

Late that summer Mother gave birth to a puny boy who Father named Arthur. He looked on the child's birth as a good omen and tried to raise Mother's spirits by claiming it meant that all his dreams would be realized. The boys as a group were a bit embarrassed to have a baby brother. After all, he was younger than Mother and Father's first grandchild, Lottie's little boy. Mother hugged Arthur fiercely to her breast and turned her back on her family. In all the excitement of the barn plans, few noticed that she rather unraveled as Arthur grew stronger and became more independent. Later the family remembered that after Arthur's birth, she never again carried even one bucket of water up from the well.

■ ■ ■

After harvest, David caught up with his father's plans on occasional weekends, as he had secured his first employment as a teacher in the one horse town of Pokerville. Pokerville's name indicated its reputation. The village had three thriving saloons when David arrived, and he learned that the menfolk played cards from noon on Saturday, throughout the night to Sunday morning, when their wives came to drag them to church.

The grimy windows of the buildings looked out on a single road that wound past squalid storefronts. Few respectable folks lingered very long in the collection of nondescript buildings that called itself a village.

Pokerville even had a dance pavilion, a clear sign of its depravity. It was a rambunctious town all right, but David discovered soon after arriving that some folks had established a Good Templars' Lodge, called "Forward 555." He joined as soon as he was asked. Later he was proud to learn that by 1879 their small group had grown to fifty members advocating and practicing total abstinence.

David settled in with William H. Jones and his family for board and room before he learned that Mr. Jones had once given a "grand ball" at the Dance Pavilion to which forty to fifty couples had been invited. Since David's family was plum set against dancing as well as drinking, he was understandably on edge for the first few days, but when he saw no dancing, he soon learned to relax and appreciate Mrs. Jones' delicious cooking.

Maintaining the classroom was a challenge. There were always lessons to plan for the sixteen students in six grades, all taught in one room. What was most difficult was keeping the room warm, clean and in order. Though he could start the fire easily enough, he hadn't had much experience with a broom. In winter David arrived early to start the wood stove, but it was usually mid-morning before students were warm enough to do any copybook work. He did have help however, for each student was required to bring in a load of wood or a pail of water upon arrival. David looked back with nostalgia at his careless school days when he took the warm schoolhouse and well-planned curriculum for granted. He had trouble reversing roles and playing the part of teacher.

There were few teacher's aids in those days. David had one forty-seven page pamphlet entitled, *Instruction in English For the use of Teachers* [sic]. It covered grades one through eight in an orderly fashion. What he followed most closely was the admonition in the "Notes" that advised, "…nothing excels a well conducted recitation." When he used the recitation method, he found himself, as well as the class, educated as well as entertained.

Fortunately, the school was removed from the main street with its rowdy element and located on the edge of town near a hill with a grove of trees and an empty prairie that was perfect for recess. In fact, recess was the best part of David's day, especially when he could go sledding with the older children while the younger ones played.

Until the class room warmed up, David kept the students busy reciting and doing board work. By noon everyone was happy to explore their lunch buckets and after some noisy jeering and food trading, they all sat down to eat. The schoolhouse was really warm by this time, and after lunch, if David was lucky, he could settle down for a couple hours of reading from the *McGuffey Reader* for the little ones and mathematics and copy work for the older students.

The hours spent in the classroom this first year were difficult at best for David, and occasionally they were torture. No matter how hard he tried to act in a mature way, his slight frame and smooth face belied his age. He assured the students he was eighteen, but not many looked as if they believed him. He attempted to grow a mustache, but the few straggly hairs he nurtured just made him look younger.

After the first few weeks he did fine with the young ones and the girls, but some of the boys were older and bigger than he was. The Arnold boys were David's worst dilemma. They had learned to spit from their father, and persisted in demonstrating their skills for the rest of the class at the most inopportune times.

As was his custom, David set the older students to work on reading and figuring while he listened to the younger children recite. The smallest of the lot stood to declaim, "D is for dog, dolly, door—" when she was stopped cold by a formidable throat clearing which ended with a stream of tobacco juice squirting across the classroom floor. The room became dreadfully silent. David glared at Lester Arnold while most of the older students just sat back and watched to see what would happen.

Mustering his courage and his deepest voice, David said very clearly and slowly, "Get up now, find your coat and leave this school!"

Seriously surprised not to be physically confronted, Lester paused before he shambled to an upright position. "You ain't tellin' me what to do." He looked around at his audience, hoping to get a laugh. "I'm leaving this chicken coop and never coming back!"

"Get your coats on for recess," David announced, hoping that Lester didn't linger around the school ground. Then he cleaned up the mess on the floor.

David found himself praying that the younger Arnold boy and his sister would get sick and stay home, but they didn't. The showdown with the Arnolds occurred because of their sister. Though only eight, the Arnold girl had developed the annoying habit of pulling the braids of the smallest students. David slapped her hand right after she made a particularly vicious yank on Abby Brochneir's hair. "Never do that again," he advised.

The Arnold girl looked back at her brother and announced, "I'll do as I please!" The two of them grabbed their coats and marched out of the schoolroom.

The next day their father, Mr. C.B. Arnold, came to school and threatened David if he presumed to discipline his children again. "You stay away from my Abby! My boys and me, we'll give you young dandy a good beating, you do it again." Arnold was bigger than David, but he did not seem to want to make good on his threat. Instead, Mr. Arnold pulled all three children out of school. It was a relief to David and the students alike. Furthermore, David was happy to discover most of his new friends in the Good Templers supported his disciplinary actions. In truth, his year at Pokerville was not much different than any other teacher's first year, but he did not know it at the time.

Chapter 7

PLANS TAKE SHAPE

Detail of wagon door arch (photo by author).

When the term finally ended and spring came, David headed home with nary a look behind. His father was pleased to have good help breaking ground for a new cornfield, and David was ready for physical work. Father had purchased a pair of oxen after they moved the house down to the new place, and the animals continued earning their keep by plowing up the prairie for new fields. Father was determined to grow corn to fatten the cattle before sending them to market.

Before settling into the spring farm routine, David had secured a teaching job in Jennieton for the fall term (1878). Jennieton was a sort of town consisting of two farm houses, a school, two carpenter's shops, a preacher's house, a church, a blacksmith's shop, and a so-called hotel which was really a combination of saloon, roadhouse, and grocery store. Crowded in with the groceries was a hat shop run by David's cousins, the Evans girls, who ordered hats direct from Chicago.

David planned to live at home so that he could save money and keep track of the barn's progress. He knew he could teach, and this year he determined to prove it close by, and he did. The Jennieton newspaper reported, "Our district school is progressing under management of DD Thomas." Indeed, the Thomas family had become rather important in the area. Father had completed one term as Justice of the Peace, and he was planning to run for the second term. Both he and the community were well convinced of his judicial ability.

Father also imagined himself to be part of a larger agricultural, economic, and political movement. While he had no reason to join the much discussed Dairymen's Association, he had been following William Dempster Hoard's career in improving dairy farming. "That man Hoard will be Governor someday," Father predicted, and he lived to see his words come true in 1889. He addressed David, "Tell me about this Stephen Moulton Babcock. Why is he fussing so much about the butter fat content in milk?"

David didn't have the answer and responded vaguely, "Maybe butter fat is important to a dairy farmer, but we're in the beef and hog business. What do you think about the farmers buying land in Mineral Point as a permanent site for the County Fair?"

Walter would have none of it. "A County Fair?" he growled, "Just plain foolishness. The only thing worth our time and interest is the railroad."

Each discussion of progress literally began and ended with the railroad. Walter and his neighbors looked forward to having a railroad at their barn doors by 1881. Newspapers promised farmers that they would no longer need to haul produce long distances over bad roads, and they would have direct communication with Madison and other commercial centers in the state and Midwest. The railroad was part of Walter's plan. He was determined not to be left behind.

There was a kind of magic in the summer of '78—the sun shone when they needed it and rain always came just in time. It looked like they would have a great harvest, and Father could not have been happier. He had been talking with bankers on and off since the first of the year. They assured him that the money would be there when he needed it. This gave him leave to begin digging for the foundation of the barn. He was excited about the project, and he tried to make David and his brothers feel that they were right there on the ground floor of something really special.

That year, the idea that the barn would become a reality rather crept up on the family. One evening early that summer when the corn was growing so fast that they could hear it take on new heights, Uncle Isaac came over with a surveyor's level. He and Walter sighted each corner ten times if they did it once. The next night was the same. They would move corner posts a fraction of an inch and then begin again. Once Walter stormed down to the well, dowsed his head with cool water and came back to double check everything once more. They were "orienting" the barn so that it lined up perfectly with the cardinal compass points.

Watching the men were Walter's five boys, comfortably sprawled on the cabin's porch and step. In reality, they were five restless young men unsure of where their future would take them and how their father's project would affect it. Only David knew he was going to school to be a lawyer. The others were adrift.

"Look at them," Tallie said bitterly, "scheming more work for us."

"Who else do ya' suppose is going to dig the bloody foundation?" Thomas growled, his face dark with pent-up frustration. Both he and Price were seriously courting young ladies from town. They were just itching to be out on their own.

Price nodded his head and announced that he had asked Father for a stake if he would stay and build the barn. Father had agreed. The others were amazed that Price had even brought up the subject of leaving. Price allowed that the stake was not much money. He said, "I figure it will get me to the gold fields where I can make a place for Flossie to come and join me."

There was quiet as they smoked or chewed and spat, thoughtfully considering Price's announcement.

"I wouldn't feel bad about working for a stake," Seth said softly. "I was talking to some drummers in Arena who said there was nothing but opportunity in Telluride, Colorado. Gold everywhere you scratched the surface of the ground." Five heads nodded slowly.

They looked again at the two older men and visualized a very large stone barn behind them. The young men saw a way to realize their own dreams. So it was that Ol' Watt built his barn and lost his boys to the lure of the gold fields.

■ ■ ■

The next day Isaac and Father rather expected the boys to begin digging the foundation. After his own talk with Father, Tallie's mood had shifted to almost giddy elation. He knew the barn was his escape route. "Digging to China, we can't deny ya. Come on boys, we're digging to China." He attacked the digging with alacrity and almost desperate determination. Joking, teasing, occasionally breaking into some crazy kind of song, he kept everyone in a good mood.

The idea was to establish the barn on bedrock. Father and Isaac believed, but could not be sure, that a solid rock table might extend under the soil to use as their foundation. Nothing could be better for a stone structure that the builders intended to last forever. Luckily they were right about the bedrock. Isaac used blasting powder in one corner to nudge some rocks loose. Then they readjusted the siting a bit so the barn would rest on a smooth shelf of stone extending out of the hillside. The north side would be completely underground while the east, south, and west foundation sides would be exposed. Such a construction was called a "bank" barn.

When they were not busy with the farming, the boys and sometimes their cousins spent the morning digging. Then everyone took as long a dinner break as he could, eating up Mother's good food and moving off quietly to catch some sleep during the heat of the day. In the afternoon, David and Price hitched up the oxen and loaded up hay wagons with dirt and rubble. These loads filled in hollows north of the house for a three-quarter mile roadway they were building to the quarry at the same time they were excavating Father's foundation.

"We'll be haulin' stone over this 'yer road come winter," Isaac advised the boys. "Make it smooth, and make it straight."

Occasionally, men from as far away as Mineral Point came to work. Father eagle-eyed the day labor and sent them packing if they loafed on the job.

The foundation, of course, was just the beginning. By mid-summer Isaac began another project. When the boys were not working in the fields or fixing fences, they used a couple of oak and steel-rimmed wheelbarrows to cart limestone gravel to the valley below the barn site where Isaac was building a lime kiln.

"What do we need with a kiln?" Thomas groused. "I thought it was a barn we was building."

Isaac patiently explained, "We burn limestone to make lime for the mortar that we will be using in the barn walls." And it could not be just any kind of quicklime, it had to be the best quality, made from the hardest limestone. Isaac would need large quantities of lime when the masons began laying up the walls in the spring, so the kiln must be in full operation by the fall.

"Now you boys can continue hauling wood for burning," Father ordered in late fall when Isaac had finished laying up the stone for the kiln. "The fire will more than likely be going all winter." Isaac had made the kiln about fifteen feet tall. David did not have to bend over much to walk into its mouth. Ignoring the boys' lack of enthusiasm for hauling firewood and stone, Isaac interrupted, "I'll be picking out the hardest stones to burn." Don't bother bringin' down the soft stuff."

While the boys sometimes felt they were being worked like the slaves who built the pyramids, Father had a way with young men. He worked them in competitive teams, and they developed strength and endurance trying to outdo each other with how much they could dig, and pull and haul.

It almost seemed that Mother and the girls might be in on the plan as well, because David could not remember when they had such good food to eat. And while the boys did not dare expect it, they did eat a lot of pie that summer. Mother and Sadie would spread the food right out on planks on the porch, and they would eat it like a picnic. Probably Father's trump card was the nap that they all grabbed after such good eating. Some days they did not get back to work until after three o'clock. David was not sure if his father planned it that way or if he overslept because Father worked right there with them every day.

Father was finally ready for the next step in his plan, hauling stone for the walls. As the weather became colder and his family gathered round the fireplace, he talked. He said that he believed barns could be pleasing objects, that they could "…impart a feeling of comfort and completeness upon all who saw them." He continued to quote Mr. Hasted, "With the increase of wealth and we may add good sense and enlarged ideas, among the farmers of the country, there is a gradual but very decided improvement in farm architecture." Isaac was right there agreeing with him. Mother left the room at the words, "good sense," and the boys began finishing off the road to the quarry the next day.

That winter Isaac showed the boys how to build their own stone boats. "Stone sleds, as some called them, have been around for centuries," he told the boys at dinner. They were really sleds, built low to the ground so large stones could be rolled or tumbled onto them. The runners were shod with iron which made them last longer and easier to pull. "Now that the road is finished, we'll just see how these work."

■ ■ ■

At the first smell of spring Father went about building that barn like he had built a dozen before it. There was a very large, perfectly oriented hole in the barn yard. It testified to the boys' hard work and Father's good luck that they had dug down to bedrock. Beside the hole was an astonishing pile of rock that the boys and Isaac had assembled during the winter. Father and Isaac completed the financial calculations, and Father mortgaged the farm.

That spring of '79 the boys and some good hands from town worked on shoring up the roadway to the quarry again. The usual quiet of summer field work was occasionally disrupted by loud explosions. When this happened, Thomas found himself working alone in the fields, for Seth and Price always managed to be on hand when Isaac got out the blasting equipment. "Why should you get to do all the exciting work?" Thomas asked.

"We're older," his brothers replied coolly, "and we might just be needing dynamiting skills when we want to blast that gold out of the western hills."

Father and Isaac used blasting power to break loose the building stones from the limestone outcropping in the quarry. They hoped to pull more loads of stone over the new road that summer.

Father estimated that it would take two years to finish the barn, what with the need to farm as well. He was about right if one did not count the planning and digging and putting on the roof. There appeared to be enough rock in the quarry three-quarters of a mile away. The road they built was satisfactory, although it needed shoring up after each big rain storm.

It was sometime around Fourth of July that Timothy from the Spring Green area came to live with the Thomas family. He was the stone builder for all the Jones clan. Everyone over there called him Uncle Timothy. Heavily bearded and more hairy than David was accustomed to, he was very gentle, and spoke in a soft, agreeable accent. "What effer," Isaac and Ol' Watt wanted, he would help.

Timothy was rather a specialist. He spent most of his time with the biggest stones, fashioning them into perfectly smooth rectangular blocks. He and Isaac would check the perfection of each face. They knew that if these corner stones, or "quoins" as they called them, were perfect, then their walls would be plumb. He also paid special attention to the smaller stones that were used for the arches. "Yer see, boys, we need to "dress" some of the most important stones. This is no shanty barn, boys, this is a cathedral barn."

Uncle Timothy and the other masons lived with the Thomases for almost three years. They built a lean-to on the back of the cabin, and they ate three meals a day with the family. Sometimes they would get rather smelly, and Mother would say, "I'm putting my foot down now. Everyone who eats here takes a Saturday night bath." She said it with a smile because she liked their stories and their songs.

During the summer of '79 Father directed Uncle Timothy to instruct the boys and half a dozen hired men in the finer points of rock stacking and rock loading. Timothy tried to frighten the boys a bit with tall tales of flying stone sleds, overloaded and unbalanced. "Start with a light load," he advised, "you can always add more as you learn." He showed them how to prepare for emergencies by cutting a couple of small logs just big enough to throw in front of the runners to stop the sled before it was out of control. One pleasure they received from doing this job was riding an occasional stone boat all the way from the quarry to the lime kiln.

At first, the boys just loaded the sleds any which way. "Oh no, that won't do." They had to restack the entire load, the thin stones on edge, wedging them tightly so they would not domino going around the last big curve. The sleds had removable boards on each side to insure that what was put on the load at the quarry, would arrive at the barn site at the bottom of the road.

That year of loading and unloading stones led to muscle development in David as well as a few aches and pains since he was teaching school and only worked on his days off. "The trick," Timothy explained, "is to keep your back straight and bend your knees when moving the big rocks." They soon learned that builders used the large stones first. They did not want to have to lift those big ones up any higher than necessary. Father insisted the crew use Timothy's technique. He did not want damaged backs, and he also did not want to waste time with injuries. Timothy often used a winch cable on the biggest stones.

The masons sorted the quarried stone as the boys brought it down. They erected boards at the corners of the foundation and ran strings from corner to corner. Working in groups of three to lay up the stone, the masons used four tools, a four-foot-long level, a plumb bob, a hammer for rock splitting, and a trowel for the mortar. One man would hand up the stone, another would haul mortar and the third would spread the mortar, and place the stone. Isaac and Timothy did most of the placing. Frequently, they paused to assess a stone, looking for its grain much as a wood splitter might look for the grain to split wood. The mason would give a mighty whack or a gentle tap and a part would drop off, leaving the rock a perfect shape for its fit in the wall.

The quoins had to be wrestled into place with the help of a block and tackle. Working a careful two-foot span at a time, the masons frequently used the plumb bob and level to determine if the wall was true.

One ordinary work day Walter approached the construction site from the north. He was driving a wagon full of supplies. As was his custom, he marveled at the meaningful activity and the ordered progress that was being made. He prepared to unload the supplies, when he heard the first whoop and cry from the quarry.

"Whoa there, Whoa."

"Look out below! Comin' down—"

"Watch out!"

"Get off the road!"

Walter, like the others, was attracted to the hollering and moved toward the quarry road. He looked up to see Seth waving his hat wildly. Price and a hired man were struggling to control the oxen. The crazed animals had been hit by the stone sled which had not been fastened adequately on one side. It had swung around and hit an ox. Cut loose by the men, the sled swiveled and swung its way almost to the barn site where it slid off the road and dumped its load of rocks. When the dust settled, the quiet was devastating. The observers were busy counting heads and praying no lives had been lost. Relieved beyond understanding, Walter was the first to speak. "We'll need a winch to reload the rocks, boys. Best set it up after lunch. Seth, see to the ox. Perhaps a poultice will keep the swelling down. It would be a pity to lose 'em."

■ ■ ■

Carpenters made frames for the doors and windows which were a special challenge because the openings were all arched. This was quite a departure from the usual method where doors and windows were planned so they extended either to the top of the wall or stone lintels were used. It was the arches that made this barn uniquely like a church or cathedral.

The construction of the arches, in three different styles, had been a never-ending source of fascination for everyone but Mother. Uncle Timothy was particularly meticulous with the key stones which were carefully shaped to protrude a bit when ultimately set in place. There was no structural value to the protrusion, it just was aesthetically pleasing.

All the laborers enjoyed the mysteries of those intricate puzzles which would be laid carefully out on the ground before being set into the wall. "Timothy," Isaac would call, "are you finished with the keystone?"

Timothy casually brought up the stone he had cut and dressed to fit, "I think this one will work," and he carefully slipped it into place.

The spectators sighed in admiration for the man and the power of this stone and its fellows to enable the walls surrounding the open space to support the tons of stone above.

The masons worked sometimes late into moonlit nights to place all the arch stones, thus ensuring that no wild animal or loose cow would knock the props out of the temporary bracing and send a pile of stone crashing down to the ground. In a couple of days when the mortar had hardened, the masons carefully removed the wooden framework, holding their breaths for what seemed like minutes, as they admired the strength and magical beauty of the arched open space.

The masons worked as late as possible into the fall. When the mortar would not hold because it was too cold, they put up their tools and supervised the stone removal from the quarry. They needed to accumulate a great deal of rock to finish the walls.

Day after day that winter it dawned crisp and cold with nary a cloud in the blue sky. They were lucky. A big snowfall could close down the operation till a thaw in January or so.

When the weather finally became impossible, Walter brought out Isaac's drawings and tried to calculate how much longer it would take to complete the barn. On clear days Father would bring Mother to the site, explaining to her some fine point of construction, or pointing out the cut stone which they had laid out to form arches over one of the many doors and windows he envisioned. She would look where he pointed and shake her head as if she could never really comprehend the amazing significance of such a project.

One particular Sunday when chores were finished and supper enjoyed, the entire family gathered near the fireplace while the snow fell steadily all around the cabin. Father explained how they would build ramps up to the walls that could be adjusted to the height of the wall. "The laborers," Father said as he looked around at the boys, "can trundle the stones up the ramp to the wall where the masons will wrestle them into place." The stone barn was entering its final stage of construction.

Chapter 8

INDIAN FIRES, 1880

Date stone. Photo by author.

It was a bright, end-of-winter day in 1880, and the farm was a beehive of activity focused on the barn when one of the hands noted the smoke from Indian fires. Walter said at first, "Pay no mind to that smoke. Injuns always burn in the spring."

He had sent the boys to town for seed. David was teaching in Jennieton, and there was only Mother, the girls, little Arthur, and himself to watch with the masons and the stone haulers as the fire crept closer and closer to their fields where they could ignore it no longer.

It became very dark. The sun was dimmed by increasing clouds of billowing black smoke. "Go to the barn," Father told Mother, who began coughing heavily as the smoke reached them.

Mother looked quickly around saying, "Margaret, find Arthur. Find your brother now." The girls began to cry as they realized their home was being threatened. One burly fellow from town assessed the situation quickly and unhitched the oxen from the stone sled.

Father directed him to the plow and hitched up the oxen, first tying a bandanna over the oxen's eyes so they could not see the flames. "Quiet, quiet now, fellows, we really need your help." Father's steady voice attempted to hypnotize the animals, "Whoa now, just move ahead like you've done before. It's only a little plowing we're doing." Heading in the direction of the sooty inferno, Father led the oxen at their head as the hired man took hold of the plow. Eventually, they plowed a wide swath on the southeast side of the house for a fire break.

The hired man punctuated Father's soothing voice with a variety of expletives as he struggled to hold the frightened animals, "Tarrrnation! Your ornery buzzards, just pull the plow!" In between invectives and against the roar of the fire, the girls could hear him shouting to the masons, "Backfires, get the backfires going." The masons looked in vain for where they could start a backfire, for the wind had shifted and was blowing the fire toward the cabin.

Mother finally recovered a bit and ordered Margaret and Sadie to move what they could from the house to the barn. "Arthur," she ordered, "you must help Margaret and do as she asks." As a construction site, the stone barn stood like a fortress, with strong thick foundation walls almost completely surrounded by bare ground and piles of quarried stone and rubble. The fire would not hurt the barn. The masons had completed breaking up the sod around the house and formed a water brigade from the well, pouring water on the roof of the cabin. They all worked for what seemed like hours until it was impossible to do anything more.

Father and the hired man were trembling as they struggled to bring the oxen to safety. Father had finally turned his back on the prairie fire and headed for the barn. "We're a comin' in!" the hired man roared, his voice hoarse with smoke and despair. He and Father unhitched the team and brought them into the lower level of the barn.

Mother and the girls had to move quickly out of the way of the frightened animals. Arthur began wailing, "Will the fire come in here with us? Where is Father? Mama—" His mother absentmindedly patted his head limply and looked sadly at her child, saying nothing at all.

Wild-eyed and as exhausted as the oxen, the girls huddled together. Mother stared dully ahead with Arthur sobbing quietly at her feet. The masons and other workers drifted in soon after and collapsed against the walls of the yet unfinished barn.

From the wide doorway of the stone barn's first level, they watched the fire approach and prayed breathlessly until the smoke forced them to turn their backs. Nimble villain that it was, the fire literally blew across the plowed space, and it only took a few sparks to ignite the roof of their home, despite the masons' attempts to wet it down.

This time Mother was not able to watch her home burn. After she and the girls rescued what they could, she had just walked slowly to where her rocker from Wales sat in the corner of the dusty barn, collapsed into it and rocked and rocked. Little Arthur stayed close, trying occasionally to crawl into his mother's lap. "Maaama!" he howled. Seeking comfort and finding none from his mother, he finally cried himself to sleep in Sadie's arms.

David and his older brothers had seen the smoke from town and came as soon as they could. By the time they arrived home, the smoke was hanging over the charred remains of their cabin. The fear almost staggered David, as he recalled the first time he had seen their home burn. "Mother, Father!" he called desperately.

"Sadie, Margaret, Arthur… ," Tallie yelled. Then they stopped as one by one, their family lined up in the wide doorway of the stone barn, and they realized no one had perished.

Mother did not cry or even talk for days. She just coughed a lot like she could not get the smoke out of her lungs. The fire and Mother's reaction to it was frightening for all the children, and even for Father. Perhaps that is why it did not seem any time at all before their next log cabin was built. That one lasted until it was torn down in 1935.

Those nights after the fire the boys and the hired men lived in the lower barn. They shared some old hay and spread it with quilts saved from the house and borrowed from the cousins. As the nights grew warmer, they enjoyed the dark coolness of the lower level where they could look up and watch the stars come out and the moon rise. There was an enchantment over those nights as they talked of their futures, told stories, and even sang a bit. They awoke with a start at the break of day, completely rested and ready to go to work after a quick wash and a swig of Mother's coffee.

Mother and the girls were making do in the granary that was almost empty at this time of year. They used an outdoor kitchen that the hired men had rigged up for them. There was an understanding that good food was essential for any progress to be made on barn or house. Therefore, everyone, Father, the boys, the masons, the hired men, helped with kitchen chores. The stove was hauled from the fire and cleaned, firewood all split and ready to be used miraculously appeared each day very near the stove. The girls never had to haul water that summer. There were always three buckets neatly covered and waiting for their use. When it came time to wash and clean up, the fellows and boys took turns helping the womenfolk. Few of the men and certainly not Walter realized that Sadie was doing most of the cooking by now.

Meanwhile, Father set about keeping his building project on schedule. "Price, you're in charge of constructing the house. The rest of you can help him. David, you work on the fireplace." The cabin was built much like their other log homes. Round logs were used that could be handled by David and his brothers. The older boys were especially helpful, as they realized they could well be building cabins out West very soon.

The new cabin was fourteen feet square with a puncheon floor which they made by splitting logs in half and laying them flat side up. They worked hard to smooth those boards, but there was no way to prevent giant splinters when they went barefoot.

The only thing they did not have to do was dig out a cellar because they built over the old home site. They did dig out the cellar more cleanly however, and built some nice shelves for Mother's preserves.

David was most proud of the fireplace which he laid up mostly by himself, following as carefully as he could Uncle Timothy's instructions. Uncle Timothy had kind of adopted the Thomases, and he was still working on the barn with the other masons to complete the walls so the roof could be finished before winter set in.

Uncle Timothy was David's favorite among the three masons. While he expected too much of David's ability to move rock, Uncle Timothy always made David feel special. He called him "Mr. David" and let him cut some of the stones that they used for the arches.

The fireplace took up most of the west wall of the house. David used the biggest field stones at the base and finished off with a mantel for Mother's clock. The stones laid up nicely. David had not built a barn, but he had learned a thing or two about how to put up rock.

Mother moved in from the granary. Looking proudly at her strong, tall sons, she said, "I'm gratified to have boys who can build such a fine home." Father complemented them as well, especially on following his suggestions for using bark slabs on the roof. That winter David enjoyed stoking the fire and keeping things toasty for the family.

While the boys had been busy with the cabin, the prairie had greened up, the hired men had planted the crops, and Father and his crew of masons had made significant progress on the stone barn. Another summer had passed, and the walls of the great barn were three-quarters finished.

Uncle Timothy was working with chisels and a hammer on a neatly cut stone. David watched for awhile as the mason painstakingly chiseled out the stone to read "188" and then Timothy turned to offer him the tool. David held the chisel carefully where Timothy had scratched another 1 in the stone, and together they completed the date—"1881." That was when the walls would be finished and when the railroad would come through. After they mortared in the special stone, all the workers sent up a cheer. Sadie came out with fresh cider and cookies and three apple pies, right there in the middle of the afternoon. It was a real celebration.

By the end of the building season, the barn was taking shape, although it was far from completed. The big arched doors on the north were stunning. Less than a quarter of the walls remained unfinished. The going was slow as every stone had to be trundled up the ramp before it was set in place, and then the ramp had to be moved and then raised again as the walls became higher.

One traveler, passing the site at twilight, spoke in hushed tones about what he had seen rising out of the prairie. He said that it appeared to be a great Greek ruin constructed by ancient heroes.

Chapter 9

HERE COMES THE RAILROAD, 1881

Ridgeway Depot.

The winter of '80-'81 before the walls were complete was difficult for Father. It snowed early and the men from town grumbled about working on the snowy slope between the barn and the quarry. The men's complaints didn't concern Father as much as a six-by-eight-inch advertisement in the local newspaper featuring a map of southwestern Wisconsin. It was run weekly by the Chicago and North Western Railway.

Walter studied it, reading aloud, "This new and correct map proves beyond any reasonable question that the Chicago and North Western Railway is by all odds the best road for you to take when traveling in either direction between Chicago and all the principal points in the West and Northwest." His boys stole quick looks at each other when they heard the word "West," but Father ignored them.

He had reason to be interested and concerned. The county was fairly vibrating with activity. It was rumored that Dodgeville was planning housing for over one hundred railroad workers. Railroad construction bosses wielded a lot of power, and were the source of much speculation and the focus of occasional anger, because fortunes could be made or lost depending on the exact route of the railroad.

The Dodgeville Chronicle recorded on December twenty-fourth that, "A railroad construction boss… known generally as Jack Stack, got into an altercation with one Mike O'Conners, of Lodi, Wis, when the latter stabbed him with a pocket knife, inflicting a wound three and one-half inches deep, between the third and fourth ribs, cutting the pericardium of the heart."

Walter realized that railroad men played rough, and he needed to take into account the railroad's need for construction hands. By May, a large quantity of ties and rails were ready and waiting in Dane County just east of Blue Mounds. Most itinerant labor chose to work for the railroad, and Ol' Watt was forced to pay competitive wages or put up with unreliable laborers for his construction project.

The boys set to work again in the spring of '81 after the masons assured Father it was warm enough for the mortar to bind. Father hired some fellows to do fieldwork, watch for the new calves, and see to the fences. He believed his boys had learned enough to be of real help to the masons this summer. Meanwhile, the trusty crew from town continued to haul stone from the quarry.

The masons knew how to pick stone and haul stone, but what they did best and enjoyed the most was laying up stone. Father was proud of them and proud of himself for hiring them for such an ambitious project. "Master craftsmen, that's what they are. That's what you need to build a fine building." Ol' Watt professed his pride to almost anyone who would listen to him in town. No one disagreed.

The masons alternately treated David and his brothers as apprentices or slaves, occasionally explaining some aspect of construction in minute detail and more frequently working them to exhaustion. If there were no problems, the masons believed they would easily finish the barn by the time the railroad came through.

When it came time for summer fieldwork, Father was so involved with barn construction that the day laborers practically managed the farm by themselves, that is, until something went wrong. Then they were set straight about who was really running the farm.

Every day, Father would walk around the building site, admiring the progress made and trying to gauge the size of the rock piles assembled around the foundation. It was as if he were willing the barn to be finished, stone by heavy stone.

Even as they neared the end of their project, Timothy and Isaac continued to lecture the laborers. "Use judgement, common sense," they advised. "Bricks are all the same, but no stone is like another one, and each one is an artistic challenge." The masons were artists, but building with stone was dirty, hard, and sometimes dangerous work.

■ ■ ■

The railroad was changing everything. The future of Jennieton was a great topic of discussion in 1881. The depots were built in Ridgeway and Dodgeville, so some felt Jennieton would become a "dream of the past" while others felt that with men like Walter Thomas, "our great stock raiser," Jennieton must not be allowed to die.

While the Thomases were busy with their barn, other folks in the area greeted progress with different kinds of enterprises. Everyone was sure that they would become rich overnight, or at least very soon. One neighbor, Mr. David Simpson gave the railroad the right-of-way for one dollar if it would build the depot on his land. He immediately began to subdivide and sell parcels of land. As soon as the deal was made with the Chicago and North Western Railroad, nine stores, one hotel, two blacksmith shops, and four dwellings were built. Homes and businesses were moved from Jennieton and Pokerville to what eventually became Barneveld.

Some folks claimed that the new town was named Barneveld at the suggestion of the railroad's Dutch surveyor in honor of his hometown in Holland. The primarily Welsh inhabitants of the new town did not care what the town was called as long as the train stopped there. In the future, the railroad men had occasion to look at this section of rail along what was commonly called Military Ridge, and recognize it as one of their most profitable sections of track anywhere.

Regular trains began running between Madison and Dodgeville after the Fourth of July. A small wood-burning engine with an oversized smoke stack pulled the first cars into town. By 1882, the schedule indicated two daily passenger trains and two or more freight trains were traveling each way. There was also a daily freight train called the "Cannonball" which left Lancaster, Wisconsin, early in the morning and pulled a passenger coach to Madison, returning late at night. However, modern conveniences do not come without incident. Some of these were humorous and proclaimed progress in a roughshod fashion.

As Tallie related one incident, he hooted and slapped his leg. "Thomas Jones' horses got scared by the engine of the construction train just past Richard Yapp's place. The horses ran away. The load of hay they were transporting was upset. Jones was cussin' some I bet."

Mother frowned when she learned the reason for his levity. "The railroad will be the downfall of us all," she pronounced gravely. "It's the work of Satan."

The boys ceased their laughter. Then, unsure of her meaning and disturbed by her intensity, they left the room.

Local events did not interest Walter's boys very much, however. They were looking at the end of their labor in Wisconsin and making serious plans to head west.

The barn walls were almost completed in time for the railroad to make its maiden journey through the towns of Ridgeway and what would eventually become Barneveld, and just in time to take the first load of steers to Chicago. "The first lot of cattle was shipped from Barneveld station on Tuesday last!" proudly announced *The Dodgeville Chronicle* October 21st, 1881. Business was booming, or about to boom, and no one wanted to be left out. According to *The Dodgeville Chronicle* of September 28th, 1881, Mr. Reese and a young partner had completed their cattle yard and warehouse in Barneveld and were "expecting good times the coming fall." Daniel Thomas had erected a Fairbanks scale of "large capacity" in Barneveld. *The Dodgeville Chronicle* reported that the scale was prepared to weigh anything "from a lamb to an elephant." James Dougherty's fine new store was nearing completion, and George Farwell was erecting a new store in Ridgeway, according to *The Chronicle*, August 26, 1881.

■ ■ ■

It was apparent to everyone but Walter that the walls of the barn might be completed, but the roof would probably be delayed until spring. The beams for the roof had been ordered for months, but had not arrived yet from northern Wisconsin, and it was mid-November. Once the ice closed the rivers, there would be nothing until spring.

David's brothers were impatient. Seth spoke for them all, "Father, we're tired of waiting. We're going in the spring."

"We'd be much obliged if we could have our stake then," Price put in. "I won't be takin' Flossie now that she is engaged to that fellow from Dodgeville, but I'm going." Their departure would leave Walter with only David who would begin law school in the fall and Arthur, a mere child.

That winter the Thomas family quietly sat back and basked in the glory of their barn. The backbreaking stone work had become a magnificent architectural landmark. The freshly quarried stone shone in the reflected light of the moon, and travelers at night claimed that the barn looked like a star from a distance.

Chapter 10

THE HIGH PRICE
OF CHANGE

Nant Y. Willen cheese factory owned by Walter Thomas and his neighbors.

Mother, never one to leave everything to the men, always managed to point out the downside of the railroad business. "Railroads bring noise and destruction," she pointed out. "It's not Christian if you ask me." She read aloud to anyone who would listen, "…a number of cattle have lately been killed on the railroad. A cow, the property of Thomas S. Reese, and a bull, the property of John C. Rundell, were both killed the same day in Struttville. A number of sheep and hogs belonging to various parties have fared likewise," according to *The Dodgeville Chronicle* of August 26th. Very few men listened to her.

David was excited by the railroad and couldn't comprehend his mother's fears. He was proud of the barn and the new cabin, but he relished every opportunity that he had to leave the farm and hobnob with city folk. Teaching had become a means to an end, which was attending the University of Wisconsin's law school.

An event of the previous year had saddened all the family, but especially David. Emma Evans, their neighbor and David's cousin, had died after a lingering illness of consumption. Emma was nineteen years old and had been, everyone agreed, an estimable young lady. As a young man of inordinate shyness, David had never shared with anyone the joy he always felt when their paths had crossed, nor did he confess how dismal her death made him feel. Like his brothers, he dreamed of leaving Wisconsin.

Tallie and Seth and Thomas actually left late winter after the new year. Father had kept their wages during the barn project, and they were ready to take their stake and head west. They were determined to locate in Telluride, Colorado, where they had their eyes set on prospecting for gold. Sister Sadie's beau had died after a farming accident the previous summer, and she decided she would go along too.

"No!" her father thundered, "That's no place for a young lady."

"And in the winter too," her mother added quietly, looking with pleading eyes at her daughter.

Sadie and Price followed their brothers in the spring. They did not even wait to see the roof completed.

■ ■ ■

The railroad went right through Jennieton. The Welsh Congregational Church was directly in its path. Father got wind of the plan and arranged to take the church down. He had a idea that he hoped would make Mother happy. What he could salvage from the demolition of the church, they could have, and with the materials, he built Mother a new house. As a result, Mother could really give the railroad credit for her "fancy" new house. The clapboards looked new with a coat of paint, but the special items like the stairway banister and some panel doors made this house almost worth waiting for. "The church's stained glass window with its curved top make this a real Christian home!" she said. The congregation decided to rebuild in Barneveld, calling their new building the Swiss Evangelical Church.

Of course, Mother had earned that house and especially the pump inside that came much later. She had been a strong woman, but small, and she seemed to have become even smaller and much slower. Two fires and nine children had taken their toll.

Early spring of 1885 Father received two letters written in December of the previous year. The one dated December 13th, from Burk, Idaho, began, "Friend Walter... my Brother... asked me to write to you and tell you all about the Death of your son." It went on to say that Price had been shot accidentally at the time of the strike in Cripple Creek. "So you Son Price Was on Bull Mountain and was carrying a rifle and the Gun fell out of his hand and Went off and Shot him through the body..." [spelling and capitalization variations are writer's]

Father shared the letter with Mother, who took small comfort in the writer's concluding words, "Pierce was a good man and Stuck up for his rights and it was on that account of him carrying the gun he is buried on Bull Mountain Colorado." Neither Mother nor Father really knew the man who signed himself, "Your Ever Friend, James McClosky." Poor Mother was mortally shaken. They hadn't heard from Price in over six months, and now he was dead. The man who wrote them didn't even know if his name was Price or Pierce.

Another letter to Lottie from their sister Sadie dated December 11th did little to salve Mother's grief and horror. This one came from Pueblo, Colorado, and began, "You may rest easy it is not true that Price was shot out here."

Some weeks later Father received yet another letter from the James McClosky who had originally written them on the first of January. McClosky reconfirmed his first letter with more details, asserting that his information came from "...good Union men jest the same as Price was and Price did not get any foul play of any kind I know the men was telling the truth..." He described the incident again, "...them and Price was together one Night on Watch I suppose. So they told one that they ware walking along and Price left his gun fall and it fell the second time and it went of and killed him." McClosky added, "Know one knew it but their Selvs and no one knew it till they told me." He finished his disturbing letter, "...at that time it was Every man for him Self in that country the Miners Was Fighting, U.S. Marchels and deputies, Sheriffs but Price was Killed accidentally by the gun falling out of his own hands….”

There seemed little question now that David's brother Price had vanished and was probably dead. They never heard from him again. This unsettling news laid grief on both Mother and Father, but Mother's heart and mind couldn't be eased. She grieved for Price and fretted constantly about Tallie, Seth, Thomas, and Sadie as well.

■ ■ ■

Then there was Margaret, mother's namesake, the youngest girl and closest to her heart. It was so difficult when Margaret took up with a boy named Evan. He was a good-looking lad, and very strong. His last name was Lewis. Evan Lewis, from over near Ridgeway, caught Margaret's eye one fall when he was part of the threshing crew. Margaret was serving the men dinner. “Another serving of potatoes, Evan?” she asked, innocently enough.

“Never say no to a lady,” Evan replied with a bold look at Margaret's pretty face. Then Mother would watch Evan walk Margaret toward the barn after every meal.

He had a clever way of charming the women and also a sly way of winning the wrestling matches he drummed up after work. Everyone called him “Strangler.”

Known out east as the “catch-as-catch-can wrestler of the world,” he regularly won bouts with purses between $500 and $3,000. His trademark hold was a kind of headlock that was actually a stranglehold. He would slip his wrist down below his opponent's ear over the carotid artery and squeeze, shutting off the blood supply to the brain and thus putting his opponent to sleep. The hold later became illegal in professional wrestling.

Not unlike other young men of the area, David followed the “Strangler's” career. David saved a story of Evan's “wrestle” in Grand Island, Nebraska, January ‘88. The fight with a fellow only identified as “the little Canada man” ran seven bouts with Lewis finally declared the winner. David had no reason to suspect that Margaret was clipping articles as well.

No one in the family thought much about it until Margaret received mail from Lewis. David had brought the mail from town and was especially curious about the postcard boldly signed, “Love Evan.”

“Are you writing him?” David asked as if he were entitled to know.

“Evan kept his promise and wrote me. It's nothing to do with you!” she blushed furiously, grabbed the card and ran to the barn.

Evan had traveled all over the country wrestling and winning most of the time with his special hold. That summer he worked for the Thomas family again putting up hay and threshing. Evan Lewis said that it was to prepare for his fight with Charles Green, but David thought it was because he fancied their Margaret.

Early spring found the family in more turmoil. Mother and Father did not like Evan. Father swore to Mother, "I'll disinherit that girl if she continues to see him."

Mother defended Margaret, "She loves the boy, Walter, but I must agree that he seems like a real 'rounder' to me." Margaret cried until she finally dried her tears and decided to leave home. She would head for Pueblo, Colorado, where Sadie and the boys had finally settled. Sadie wrote that there was plenty of opportunity for Margaret out there, and she would be with family. Mother then took up the crying and couldn't even help Margaret pack. When her namesake boarded the train headed west the next day, Mother was not there to wave good-bye.

■ ■ ■

David, by now a capable and confident teacher, was relieved to escape his parents' grief by teaching school. He had been busy teaching in Ridgeway that winter. He convinced the Ridgeway School Committee that he should receive thirty-five dollars per month (twenty days constituting a month), and he believed that would go a long ways toward his tuition at the University next fall.

It was 1891, ten years after the barn was finished, and most folks had almost become accustomed to the trains' noisy passage through their communities. David was involved with school, and the infrequent letters from his brothers and sisters out west indicated opportunity, always opportunity and not much more. Father stayed busy. February of that same year Father and his neighbors gathered to sign an indenture which provided they would cooperatively build a cheese factory under the firm name and style of Nant Y. Willen Cheese.

Not one to slow down, in October Walter became part of a committee appointed to raise one hundred twenty dollars to repair the schoolhouse. He, J.D. Jones, and O.C. Waus were directed to tear down the small old chimney, build a new chimney sixteen inches square, put in a new floor, and whitewash the entire schoolhouse. All this, of course, without going over budget. Most significantly, Father had accumulated almost one thousand acres of land that he owned or rented and worked. He had his barn, and Mother had her clapboard house. They should have been happy.

Father complained to David, "Your mother is spending too much time in town helping Lottie with the grandchildren."

David knew how content his mother was in town, "We do just fine by ourselves," he said. "Let her be."

Father had his way and mother came back to the farm. It went well for awhile, but it didn't last.

Mother had grown increasingly quiet. She never ventured to discuss the farm business, and she certainly never offered advice. She seemed to be listening for Price's footsteps or waiting for Margaret's pert figure to bound up the porch steps.

David wondered if she did not seek their presence in the stone barn. While she no longer took part in the difficult farm chores, she always found time to go to the barn. Every day, it seemed, she found it necessary to go down there for something. Strangely enough, the barn which had consumed so much of the family's energy, was providing a refuge for their grieving mother. The only time David ever saw her cry was in the barn.

He found her when he was hunting rats. The farm had been troubled with the varmints, and David was determined to combine target practice with the pleasure of getting rid of vermin. One afternoon when graining the horses in the barn's lower level, he heard the light scurrying of what he believed were rats above in the haymow. He went to the house for his gun and headed quietly to the barn, where the door stood just ajar. Cautiously he moved forward, gun cocked, ready for the little rodents. He looked into the half-light of the almost full barn.

"God Almighty," he breathed. There, partially burrowed in the hay almost twenty feet away was not a varmint, but his mother, drowning her muffled sobs in their old sofa pillow.

He had swung the gun up to shoot when his hand began trembling violently. He brought his other hand up to it to stop the trembling motion as he stepped back, too frightened and too disturbed to do or say anything. He knew then that Mother could not go on this way. Lottie agreed to take their mother to live with her and her family in town.

Chapter 11

BECOMING A LAWYER
1891-1895

Barneveld Fourth of July Celebration.

Finally, David had saved the tuition to begin law school at the University of Wisconsin in Madison. He was lucky enough to be taught by some of the best legal minds of the time. David's favorite teacher was Dean Edwin Bryant, a fatherly man, who delighted in David's progress.

In fact, the law class of 1895 was made up of an exceptional group of young men. Even university historians claimed the class was special. They believed at that time the student body was "hardly less important than the faculty in making the law school what it was." That may be one reason that later on the Board of Regents of the university established the David D. Thomas Law Scholarship Award in Honor of the Law Class of 1895.

In Madison, miles away from Barneveld and its local politics, David was immersed in studies and continued to be a bystander in the political foment of state politics and social issues rampant in the capital city.

However, David worked on the farm during the summer. He regularly attended the local farmers' meetings and was elected president of The Farmers' Institute to be held in Barneveld January 16th and 17th in 1892. *The Barneveld Register* later reported that the Institute was a very successful event with a large attendance of farmers who came to listen to lectures about "Cattle and Swine Breeding," "Dairy," and "Will it Pay to Build a Silo?" At the evening session David himself gave the address of welcome.

David's father increasingly turned to him for opinions on the temperance issues that were heating up political arguments all over Wisconsin and the Midwest. "Strong drink is the potion of the Devil," his father would growl. "We wouldn't have any poor folk if we shut down the saloons. What do those folks in Madison think about temperance?" he asked.

David enjoyed the respect his father gave him on topics of this nature. "Father, you know how the schools are funded. We tax the saloons. We can't just close saloons without finding another way to fund the schools. That will mean taxes on something else. What will that be?" he asked his father.

In 1893, David found himself, in spite of his preoccupation with studies, more involved with his hometown. He was approached by the city fathers of Barneveld to give the 4th of July oration. They were proud of their native son attending the university, agreeing among themselves that he "spoke like a book," but they were especially interested in something that had happened on the Thomas farm the summer before. The Thomases had made an astonishing discovery.

It happened in a strange fashion. The men were threshing wheat when the steam engine ground to a halt. "Water," the engineer called to his crew, "no water, no steam for power."

Walter directed them to the simple solution, a nearby spring. David organized an assembly line using cream cans to fill the boiler with water from the spring. Again, the engineer fired up the boiler and, NO steam! "Thunderation," the engineer shouted.

The tired crew walked over to the spring muttering other things under their breath. Only then did they notice white flakes crusted on the rocks. Ultimately, the cranky crew concluded that the water was "bad."

"I'm getting water from our well," David announced, and set off by foot to hitch up a wagon. Meanwhile, the engineer drained the boiler and everyone rested, tipping their hats over their faces against the sun. When David returned with the water, they filled the boiler. The water boiled, the steam developed, and they finished the threshing. Later David determined to ask some of his university classmates to find out what was in the spring water that caused it not to boil.

The answer was *lithium*, a soft, silver-white metallic element. *Lithium carbonate*, slightly soluble in water was used by doctors to treat bipolar disorder or mania. "Eureka!" shouted David's friend, "You can build a spa."

"Just like Waukesha," David responded dryly. "We'd call it The New Bethesda Springs in Barneveld." He paused. "It might be something to look into." They had all seen the postcards depicting the beautifully appointed buildings that had sprung up around the spring in Waukesha, Wisconsin. The most popular postcard showed a high and imposing white gate of ornate spindles through which one entered to secure a room in the elaborate Victorian home/hotel replete with towers, turrets, porches, and lots more white gingerbread. Folks flocked to Waukesha to "take the waters" and enjoy the beautiful little town.

At home Father listened to David's enthusiasm. "I won't say nay," he said, "but I won't say aye, either. You need to give me more information."

Word spread of the spring and David's possible plans. Perhaps that was why he was asked to speak on the 4th of July. He accepted the invitation formally saying that he was, "greatly honored and gratified." Privately, he was somewhat taken aback, for he believed himself to be a rather shy man not given to speaking in front of crowds. Nonetheless, he had the draft of a speech ready by the end of spring term.

David saved an article from the local newspaper covering the momentous day which was acclaimed, "A Perfect Success in Every Particular." On Tuesday, the 4th of July, 1893, the citizens of Barneveld awoke to "discharging of anvils" and "slow continual rain." Fortunately by 11:00 the air had cleared, the dust settled, and "Bunting and flags were displayed without stint." Excitement mounted with the crack and fizz of fire-crackers at every corner in the little town. By one o'clock the streets were lined with citizens and visitors, and the parade began at the Odd Fellows Hall.

David marched with the other speakers behind the Barneveld Cornet Band. They were followed by the "Car of Liberty" in the form of a beautifully decorated chariot carrying a lovely young lady dressed as Goodness of Liberty with a waving flag at her side. Drawing the chariot was a span of ponies led by the parade marshal. About fifty school-boys and girls, dressed in red, white, and blue followed. After marching through the streets, they ended at the band-stand where the exercises began with music. The marshal opened with a brief but stirring speech. Because of the late start, the officials dispensed with reading the "Declaration of Independence" and called upon David to commence with his oration.

He began, "A lovelier land Heaven's daily sun does not shine upon." Then he moved directly to the potential wonders of their spring, "Lithia." "With hopeful auguries of further developments; bidding fair to compete with Waukushau [sic.] in medicinal water of late discovered here and in becoming a place of summer resort." Then he directed the audience's attention to Blue Mounds. "Oh! How symmetrical yet how unsymmetrical!" It wasn't until much later when he reread the oration, that he was struck with its obscure phrases and pompous tone.

Not content to leave his audience without something to ponder, he traced the history of the previous one hundred and eighteen years of their glorious country. He left no historical or patriotic stone unturned, quoting Daniel Webster, lauding George Washington, mentioning Hamilton, Jefferson, Franklin, Madison, Jay, and John Marshall. Then he reviewed all the wars from the Revolutionary through the Mexican and Civil War, as well as the acquisition of territory.

He also compared the economic and social scene in America with the remainder of the world over the last two centuries. Finally, he concluded with these immortal lines by Longfellow:

Sail on O! Union strong and great!
Sail on nor fear to breast the sea!
Our hearts our hopes our prayers our tears
Our faith triumphant o'er our years
Are all with thee—are all with thee.

The newspaper reported that "Mr. Thomas was listened to with the closest attention. His remarks were appropriate and well chosen, and his familiarity with the history of our good country showed originality and possession of the loftiest wisdom and most sincere patriotism."

The visions in David's oration were as close as "Lithia" came to competing with Bethesda Springs. The Thomases built no beautiful hotel with wide verandas, and neither did they make a penny from Lithia Spring. Many years later, David did build a holding tank by the spring for the cattle—it wasn't even close to being a spa.

■ ■ ■

In 1895, David received his degree and passed the boards for the practice of law in both the circuit and supreme courts of Wisconsin. It was a pleasure to see his full name spelled out on the certificate, *David Darius Thomas Esq. of Barneveld.* Graduation day was January eighth, cold and blustery, but very, very satisfying to David and his family. His graduation picture shows him to be serious, with sandy hair brushed to one side and a bushy mustache. He had always favored a mustache, and often waxed it, as did some of the dandies of the day.

DAVID GOES WEST
1895-1900

David's graduation photo.

It seemed natural for David to head west after graduation. Thomas was in the Dakotas, farming with his wife and their growing brood of children. Tallie, Seth, Sadie, and Margaret were in Pueblo, Colorado. Tallie's letters made their life seem very exciting. In fact, it appeared to be just the place for a bright young lawyer like himself to begin practice. David had been assured that he would find it no problem to earn money on his way west by teaching school.

Father did not talk with David much about his desire to head west and rather ignored David's plans to leave. "I will need a new hired man," Father finally said quietly. "Lots of work this summer." On the day David was to leave on the train, he found his father in the hayloft of the stone barn. Father spoke slowly and almost bitterly, "You and your brothers, all gone. Only Arthur now, and he is not a farmer."

There was no answer to this. David nodded, "Yes, Father, I'll write." With his mother it was much the same, except that she could not help weeping.

At the depot, Lottie squeezed him tightly to her and said, "Go west young man! Find your fortune and a good wife. I would do the same in your place. Don't worry about Mother and Arthur." David shook Arthur's hand, saying, "Study hard, boy." Then he shook hands with his father and hopped on board the train.

David first settled in Iowa to teach a term and earn some money. It was very easy to get hired as a teacher. The first day he realized why. Few teachers could last long in the classroom with real tough gun-toting cowboys and a mixture of seven through twelve-year-olds. It almost seemed like he was reliving his first year in Pokerville. Some big strapping fellows got the best of him before he realized what was happening, and he found himself locked in the outhouse.

"Woo, Woo, Mr. Thomas, you'll have plenty of time to prepare for classes in there. We're going fishing!"

David could hear them laughing outside the door as they nailed it shut. That was bad enough, but the silence that followed when they all left for the creek was terrible.

He pushed his feet against the door with no success. Looking desperately around, he realized there is very little one can use as a tool in an outhouse. The odor became more disgusting as he contemplated staying any length of time. These thoughts fueled his determination to tip the whole house over. Unfortunately, it was fairly new and quite well-constructed. To his credit, he made so much noise with his efforts to break his way out, that a neighbor came by to see what had happened.

"Yup, I kinder suspected ye might be in a fix when the little ones came home so early." The neighbor did not seem at all surprised to find him in such a predicament, leading David to surmise that other teachers had been similarly served.

After this inauspicious beginning, he kept his gun on his desk in plain sight while he was teaching, and he only taught for a short term in Iowa and again in Nebraska. Saving almost every cent he earned, and keeping his sights on practicing law, he readily accepted all invitations to join his students' families for a meal.

From that point on, even when not teaching, he carried a revolver while he was in the West. It was a .45 Webley six-shooter. He kept it all his life. Luckily, he never had to fire it at anyone.

David took in Pike's Peak and other sights on the way. He worked part of a term in Telluride where town folk were always looking for mature gentleman teachers, especially ones who could handle a gun. He enjoyed the scenery, but did not waste too much time getting to Pueblo. It was wonderful to see Tallie and Seth again. They hugged him and pounded his back, calling him little brother and laughing like hyenas. Then Sadie and Margaret stepped forward, and he enveloped them in his arms with relish, Sadie's plump figure almost obscuring Margaret's tiny frame. Pushing them away to get a good look, David said, "Sadie, you look like a comfortable old married woman!" And to Margaret he smiled, brushed her tan cheek with his hand and said, "This climate becomes you, little sister." For a moment it was like they were all back home in Wisconsin, except Thomas had gone to North Dakota and Price was dead.

David was lucky to be able to move in with his sister Sadie, now Mrs. Sarah Buck. Her husband had fought in the Civil War and was considerably older than she was, but he made a good home for her and they had good times. Sadie was a member of the Royal Highlanders, Castle number 149. She enjoyed being active in the community. Like Mother, she was never one to sit back.

The second day he was in town, he had an opportunity to test his grit. David encountered large police dogs whose owners watched out their hotel windows for newcomers who might be carrying gold. "Bark, bark, BARK." David turned, alert but not really afraid until he heard a low growl and realized the dogs were coming closer, cornering him.

David positioned himself with his back to a building. The dogs were accustomed to intimidating newcomers. The owners showed up after the ornery dogs had thoroughly frightened their prey and looked for an opportunity to relieve David of any gold he carried. "I say, Greenhorn," one leered, "our dogs don't like you, lessen' you might have a little gold dust to brighten their day."

Laughing uproariously at what they believed was an amazingly clever ploy, the men urged the dogs forward. David surveyed the threatening curs and their cowardly owners, brandished his revolver, and let off one shot in front of them.

The dogs immediately retreated, leaving their owners no recourse but to skedaddle. David was proud to have survived so easily his first brush with the "Wild West."

■ ■ ■

It wasn't very long before David was admitted as an "Attorney and Counselor at Law" in Colorado. That was January 30, 1896, and he could practice law in Colorado for four years. As it happened, he would not need more than four years.

Letters from the farm were infrequent, but Father seemed determined to keep him abreast of his farming and business plans. David enjoyed being his confidant. Father was permanently etched in his brain as a dark, weathered figure framed by the wagon entrance to the stone barn. After sharing the home news with his brothers and sisters, David would immediately write back to his father.

He told of the boys' mining exploits, minimizing the risks they took and elaborating on their successes. In each letter he wrote, he tried to comment on Father's endeavors. Father had no one else, really. Mother was poorly, Thomas was in South Dakota, Margaret with them in Pueblo, and Price was dead. Arthur never considered farming and had headed for Chicago after graduating from Dodgeville High School. David was Father's only sounding board. It was pleasing for him to discover that after all those years, his father valued his advice.

The brothers would gather Saturday nights at Sadie's, where Margaret was living. They enjoyed a home-cooked dinner and shared family memories. This careless, comfortable frontier life continued for too short a time. Margaret became ill and had to go to the hospital where she died. David and his brothers could not really understand why she died, for she had always enjoyed perfect health. Only after the funeral did they recall some female problems that she and Sadie had tried to take care of themselves.

June 18, 1898, Sadie sat down to inform her father and mother of the details of their youngest daughter's death. The black bordered letter explained that Margaret had a tumor of the womb, which caused her illness. Although as Sadie wrote, "Margaret had been operated on at the Sisters Hospital on Saturday last, and appeared to be getting along well, but by Monday, death came upon her, and she was buried on Wednesday."

Two months later David received a telegram telling them of Mother's sudden death as well. The young people were numb as they prepared for the journey home. Mother was sixty-four years old. The train ride seemed terribly long. Tallie and Seth reminisced about Mother's strength, about how she could carry those three buckets of water at one time. David could not get the picture of his mother sobbing in the barn out of his head. They buried her in Barneveld's White Church Cemetery and erected a four-foot monument in her honor.

Chapter 13

FATHER'S DEATH
1900

Ol' Watt Thomas

It was 1899 and the country was in an increasingly boisterous spirit of celebration as the year wound to its conclusion. Not to be outdone by any other state in activities to usher in the new century, there was celebrating all over Wisconsin. Wisconsinites welcomed the dawn of the twentieth century by ringing bells, discharging firearms, visiting neighbors, and attending parties and religious services. In addition, many national figures came to Wisconsin at the turn of the century. William Jennings Bryan spoke at the Jefferson Club in Milwaukee, President McKinley spoke for ten minutes in Barneveld on his train tour through the Midwest, and Theodore Roosevelt opened the Republican campaign at LaCrosse.

News articles reflected on the great progress experienced during the nineteenth century and the glorious prospects for the coming century that were to transform American life, including technological advances in the railway, steamboat, electric motor, telegraph, sewing machine, and electric light. *The Dodgeville Chronicle* cautioned in December 28th, 1900, "…were a prophet to foretell an advancement in manners, morals, learning and social and material progress for the next century equal to that of the last he would certainly be set down as a dreamer."

■ ■ ■

There was not much celebrating on the Thomas farm, however. It was not because Ol' Watt did not believe in drinking and dancing, but because he was now alone on the farm, and feeling poorly. The previous September Walter had made out his last will and testament. Lottie checked on him now and then, but by this time he was suffering from a sore on his lip. He had been doctoring his lip for some time now with no real satisfaction. "Watt," the doctor said sternly, seeking to look directly in the old man's eyes, "this is no ordinary sore, and you need to go to Chicago where the experts can cut it out and make sure that it does not come back."

At the word "cut," Watt's shoulders straightened, and he said, "No operation for me. I've got hay to put up." And that settled the issue for the time being.

The sore had been particularly annoying because it was just where he had liked to rest his pipe. It seems these days that he could not get a good smoke without aggravating that spot. The sore did not get better, and it eventually became an enlarged and ugly lump.

At the doctor's insistence, Walter finally decided to take the railroad trip to Chicago for an operation that he hoped would cure the problem. By then his lip was very swollen, and his face looked splotchy. It was difficult for him to eat solid food. The only comfort he could get now was sipping cold soda pop through a straw. Lottie accompanied her father on the long journey, acting as a sort of human shield to protect him from the startled stares of fellow passengers. It was blistering hot on the ride to Illinois. Every time the train started up and stopped, Walter was jolted and rolled from side to side. Considerably weakened and mortally discomfited, Walter arrived in Chicago. Lottie was exhausted and feared the worst. Arthur was there to meet them with an ambulance.

At the hospital, the nurses made Walter comfortable, and he was operated on the next day. The doctors ultimately shook their heads and attempted to sew up his face. By this time, the cancer had spread beyond their ability to remove it.

Lottie and Arthur came to their father's room the next day and found him drugged with morphine and breathing very shallowly. Ol' Watt died later that evening far from home and his beloved stone barn. He was seventy-three. Before they left Chicago, Arthur sent telegrams to the family members in Colorado, North Dakota, and Wisconsin. Arthur and Lottie brought his body home on the train. Once home, Arthur lost no time arranging for the burial and funeral.

David and his brothers were devastated when they heard the news of Father's death. They clung to Sadie for comfort. Father had been forever strong, a force in their lives that they couldn't imagine not having. Then there was the farm and the stone barn. While they didn't want to be farmers, they didn't want to lose the farm either. Father had owned four hundred acres from the shot tower in Spring Green down to the present location south of the railroad tracks. He had talked about owning a thousand head of cattle.

The church service was respectful and worthy of Ol' Watt's place in the community. Evan Evans, who was the executor, decided to wait until Sadie and her brothers arrived to open the will. Meanwhile, Arthur and Lottie selected a fine monument for Father.

Soon after the family from the West gathered, they visited the grave site and agreed that the monument was impressive and appropriate. "It looks like it's befitten' of our father," Tallie announced when Arthur pointed out their selection. It was all of four feet high and eighteen inches wide.

"I've been thinking of a suitable inscription," David added. They agreed to have it inscribed:

Standing on this monument of time,
as honored, charitable, and industrious—
thus teaching to man and one God.

Next they went back to the farm to read Father's will. Father had left Thomas, Arthur, and David $2000 each. To Taliesen he left $1500. For Seth, there was $500, for Sadie "the use of $2000," and Lottie received $1000. After taking care of the specified obligations in the will, there was little cash left for the monument they had selected. It took a good deal of David's savings at the time, but he never regretted the decision to pay for the monument and honor his father appropriately.

David began work on his father's estate by sorting out the loose ends. To begin with, there was the harvest. The hired men had done what they could, but it was apparent that the farm had been neglected for many months. It was well into winter when David finally was able to set Father's business to rights, and by that time, he was once again tied, in many ways, to the farm and the stone barn. He decided to stay in Wisconsin for the time being.

Over the next few years, he enjoyed seeing the big barn filled to the rafters with hay. He saw to it that equipment was in good repair. It was always cleaned and put away carefully for the winter. He even found himself dreaming about buying more property, expanding the beef herd to eight hundred and developing a dairy herd. It was 1905 when he woke up to realize that Barneveld, Wisconsin, was his home, and the farm and the stone barn were his destiny. The next day he arranged to purchase the farm from the family, all three hundred and seventy-five acres. He was forty-five years old.

Chapter 14

THE HOUSEKEEPER
1908

Lena is the young woman seated on the right.

In the eight years since Father's death, David had almost paid off the mortgage and banked good profits. He had even purchased the mineral rights to the farm and was looking into the lead mining prospects. Out west his brothers were having luck with their gold mining. Their success inspired him with the belief that he just might find a rich vein of lead on the farm property. During late afternoons when most chores were finished, he walked the fields and woods looking for lead plants. These silvery, feather-like plants were said to grow in crevices that hid the ore. In the fall his heart pounded with excitement when he spotted the tiny lavender spires of the lead plant's blossom. He found them many places on the prairie. Eventually, he hired a first-rate dowser to come out to check some sites that he suspected might be worthwhile. The dowser cut a forked sapling from the green willow down by the old spring and gave it a try. The two of them covered upwards of five miles before the dowser advised David, "Mr. Thomas, my suggestion to you is to concentrate on farming and forget mining lead."

■ ■ ■

David's disappointment in the mining prospects of his land was just a part of a general malaise that he began to suffer. He found that he was increasingly unhappy, often downright irritated, and thoroughly bored with the life he was now living. The house was dirty and messy despite his efforts to keep things tidy. There never was enough time for housework after field and barn work, nor did he have any real inclination to do it. He had no social life except for Lottie's family and the cousins next door who occasionally invited him to Sunday dinner.

The meals that he was eating most days were eternally depressing. David could make oatmeal for breakfast, but the look of it sitting on the stove at lunch was disgusting. He found himself thinking about eating at the saloon in town with all the drummers and bachelors. When visiting Lottie, he explained, "Although the food there is passable, the company is not stimulating, and I always suffer from heartburn the next day." Lottie smiled in sympathy, and then insisted that he advertise for a housekeeper. "You old bachelors need good cooking as much as a married man does. A housekeeper could do your laundry too. We wouldn't have to look at your dingy linen and worn shirt collars. We would come to visit more often if the house was clean, and we could find a free place to sit down."

David finally agreed. When he wrote Arthur what he had done, Arthur wrote back, carefully describing what qualities he should look for in a housekeeper.

"Now David," he said, "you don't want just anyone to keep your house. You want to get your money's worth. After all, ten dollars a month is a lot of money, and you're offering her a nice warm room and board. Be sure that she is not too pretty, and not so young as to be wanting to go "sparking" with the young fellows in town. Go for strong. You don't want one of those fainting consumptive types."

The newspaper advertisement had been out for one day when David came in from chores, muck up to the top of his boots and hay in his hair, to find a farm wagon pulled into the house yard. Planted firmly on the wagon seat was the biggest woman he had ever seen. "You the man what placed this advertisement?" She shook the newspaper in his face. He nodded dumbly, taking in her strong square shoulders, her sturdy boots, and her bristly face.

I think that Arthur would approve of this one, he thought.

"I do not keep house for nobody, 'less they treat me respectful. The name's Sutcliff, Mrs. Sutcliff, and I expect a day off each month to visit my daughter in Arena." After that declaration, she rolled off the wagon and headed toward the house, a walking nightmare. David pictured day after day waking up to the smell of her coffee and the taste of her biscuits.

"No," he almost shouted, in his best lawyer voice, desperate to forestall her advance on his home. "I mean, I have not made up my mind. Someone else is coming out this afternoon. You seem qualified. Please allow me to contact you if the position is indeed open."

He had regained his dignity, and she backed away now, heading for her wagon. "I stay with my daughter. Her husband's name is Morris, Thaddious Morris in Arena," she said thickly. "You can find me there." David was surprised to discover how much the prospect of living in the same house with a woman like Mrs. Sutcliff disturbed him. A woman like that wouldn't give a man any peace. He saw her square her shoulders as she moved her horse and wagon down the road. She did look strong.

Over a cold supper that night he thought of Colorado, of his friends and family, and of the lively life in Pueblo. He needed a housekeeper, but he did not need Mrs. Sutcliff. That night he prayed for the Lord to send him another candidate, one that would not give him lumps in his stomach as well as in his throat.

David had to go to town the next day, so after chores he cleaned up, even putting on his second best coat since he needed to make a mortgage payment at the bank. After doing his banking, he stopped at the store to pick up some supplies, but mostly to plague his maiden aunts who ran the adjoining hat store. "Why don't you carry men's hats?" he teased Sadie

Evans, holding one of her confections over his head. "These are just too fancy for my taste. If you carried bowlers, just imagine the stream of young men who would come to your counter. You would have to beat them off with your umbrellas."

Sadie stared at him a moment, and then convulsed with laughter, "David, you would make a mighty handsome girl if it weren't for you being a man with a big bushy mustache and all. Quit your foolishness and sit awhile so we can discuss important things like how you are doing out there all by yourself."

"I'm doing just fine, and I have decided to hire a housekeeper," David said.

Sadie Evans was not one for beating around the bush. That was one of the things David liked about her. She had already read the newspaper and had discovered his advertisement. She said, "I know just the girl. She's from Switzerland and lives over in Amacher Hollow. I hear tell that she went to school and can speak English really well. Carrie was talking about her the other day, saying she was a hard worker and looking to hire out."

David sat up and looked closely at Sadie, not to be misled by anything. "Do you know anything about her cooking?" and then he asked cautiously, "What does she look like?"

"Lena is her name. She's a hard-working Swiss miss. I don't know anything about her looks or her cooking. Carrie said that she had been working in New Glarus, but she didn't fancy that much close work, inside. Why don't you go over to Amacher Hollow and see if she is interested?" David decided to take her advice.

The cabin at Amacher Hollow was peaceful when he arrived. Swiss dialect filled the air in what sounded like half song, half speech. After he knocked however, all became quiet, and the door opened to reveal a single room bursting with furniture and family.

"*Ja, ja*, welcome, thank you," an old lady looked him over, nodding and smiling, and beckoning him in, clearly at the end of her limited English vocabulary. She drew another person forward, pushing her toward David. "*Fraulein*—Lena." She presented the girl. Lena, wearing heavy glasses, looked to be in her mid-twenties, modest, and neatly dressed. At first he thought the girl was dumb, but she finally blushed and asked in a quiet voice what they could do for him. He was surprised to hear how good her English was. Later David learned that Lena had been in this country for less than five years, but had made good use of her time going to school and working outside.

"I need a housekeeper," David blurted out, a little discomfited by the old women's continued examination of him. Clearly they were not used to visits by lawyerly gentlemen dressed in their second best coats. "My cousin at the hat store in town thought that Lena might be interested in the position of housekeeper. I thought we could talk about it if she were available."

"I'm Lena," the girl said shyly, blinking nervously behind her glasses. "What is it that you would be requiring?"

"I need a clean house." David had never seen such glasses on a girl before. Heavy and thick, they hung on her young face like a plague. "Oh, yes, can you cook?" He managed to come out with the most important question.

Behind those glasses he thought he could see her eyes light up with confidence, "Ja, ah Jas, yes," she said firmly, "*Mutter*, my school, taught me very well, and my *kuchen*, pies, always win prizes." Throughout this the old lady and man beamed and nodded, looking back and forth between them.

With a start, David realized then that they were Lena's parents. Lena was able to speak English, and David could see as his eyes became accustomed to the cabin light that she was tall enough and strong looking, though not really a big woman.

Rather belatedly the old lady pushed a chair forward and motioned David to sit down. Lena adjusted her glasses and picked up a baby who had been sleeping until this moment. Holding the infant, she sat down across from David and asked, "What do you pay?" Arthur's advice was furthest from his mind as David negotiated with Lena and the old man and woman. It was clear that the old couple would be relieved to have fewer mouths to feed, but it was also apparent that Lena was precious to them, and they wanted her to be happy in her new position. The infant cooed peacefully during the entire negotiations.

David found himself swept into an arrangement that would begin the next day. The sing-song language, the friendly warmth of the cabin and the smell of delicious baking bread coming from the hearth oven overwhelmed his calculations and reservations. He shook hands all around and rose to leave, not realizing the momentous decision he had just made.

At home he found himself straightening up the place in preparation for Lena, the housekeeper. Arthur would have laughed, but then Arthur was in Chicago. David was a farmer in Barneveld, Wisconsin, and he was tired of coming home to a mess after a long day in the fields. He was hungry for good hot meals, and he hankered to have someone to say "Howdy" to besides the hired men.

The next day her father brought Lena in the sorriest-looking farm wagon David had ever seen. The horses, though, were a matched pair, fine looking and certainly well cared for. There was a small trunk in the back, and sitting beside the father was the girl, clutching the baby he had taken little notice of the day before. The girl would not take up much space, that was for sure, but the baby was another thing. Now Arthur really would have something to complain about. "His name is Thomas," she said stepping carefully down from the wagon.

After fetching her belongings and showing her the bedroom, David muttered, "I'll be finishing my fieldwork now." Then he turned to her, attempting to see her eyes through the thick glasses, and said firmly, "I expect dinner at seven sharp." Arthur would have been proud of him for that decisive statement.

David had a lot to think about that afternoon, but by six-thirty when he came in to wash up, overwhelmingly, his thoughts were of food. Lena did not disappoint him. They had chicken and dumplings just as his mother would have cooked them. And then there was an apple pie-like dessert that washed down with real fine tasting coffee.

"We get up early," he advised her, determined to keep a good thing going, "It would be well to come back after morning chores to a hot breakfast."

As she came to pour more coffee, Lena asked, "And when might you be comin' in?"

"Around eight," David replied, opening the newspaper.

Then Lena sat down quietly and waited until he gave her his full attention. "I'll water be needin' for cleaning, lots of water," she said. "Perhaps, the hired men be bringin' some extra buckets." David nodded assent and went back to his paper. He was wary of letting her think she could have everything she asked for, although he would not stand in way of a clean house.

Chapter 15

THREAT FROM
THE WEST

The boys' mining camp.

The year was 1910, two years after David had hired his housekeeper. It seemed like the days flew by on golden wings after Lena and Tommy came to live on the farm. The place looked good, and David felt great. Even the hired men seemed to get things done faster and better. It did have something to do with the fact that these men regularly ate their meals with David. They never tired of praising Lena's good food, especially her bread. She baked twelve loaves of *brot* at a time, and more often than not the batch was finished before the week was out. David learned to gently tease Lena when she slipped into Swiss words, so when he was near she would say, "Brooooootd," slipping from Swiss to English.

In her quiet but persistent way, Lena transformed her kitchen from a dingy back room into a bright exciting space always full of tantalizing smells and delicious flavors. She had the walls painted white and then she saw to it that all her crocks and tin-ware were neatly stowed on open shelves where she could see them and reach them easily. Eventually she had her sister make simple white muslin curtains which she always kept pushed back during the day to let in as much light as possible.

Her prize was the pie safe which she rescued from the shed where the men had used it to store spare parts for equipment. It had delightful designs punched in the tin panels of the doors for ventilation and to keep out the flying insects. She kept saucers filled with water under the legs of the safe to keep the ants away. It gave her a special kind of pleasure to line up her freshly baked bread and *kuchen* on the shelves, knowing they could cool safely without attracting insects.

One evening after dinner, David opened a letter from Tallie. After reading it he announced to Lena, "My brother Taliesen will be coming for a visit, and he wants me to invite Arthur as well." Like some men of prosperity at this time, Tallie had a private railroad car which he planned to use for the trip. He loaded it up with his brother and sister, his wife and children, and a Chinese cook. They planned to park the railroad car on a siding in the north pasture of the Thomas farm. David beamed at Lena as he explained all this to her.

She turned to get the coffee pot as she couldn't meet his eyes and replied quietly, "*Ya*, we will be ready for them, Westerners." David failed to register on her lack of enthusiasm in the face of what she viewed as an alien invasion.

The two of them spent long hours preparing for the visit. Lena would be proud to open the house to them. David looked forward to showing the visitors improvements on the farm. He made a special effort to clean around the stone barn, even asking the hired men to put a fresh coat of green paint on the louvers.

■ ■ ■

Finally, "They're here!" David called into the kitchen on the appointed day. The engineer had uncoupled the beautiful car in the north pasture just below the bridge where railroad workers had put in a temporary siding. Alerted by the impatient steam whistle, David and the hired man hitched up the wagon and rushed to the pasture. In his excitement David completely forgot to pick up Lena and Tommy who trailed along on foot.

The car was big and seemed even bigger as the train pulled slowly away. Painted dark green with yellow and gold trim, it reminded David of a circus wagon. As soon as the chocks were set against the track, the folks rushed out, Sadie, Seth, Tallie and his beautiful wife, their children, and the Chinese cook.

"Welcome, welcome to your Wisconsin family home," David said and could say no more. Taken aback with feelings for his family, he limited himself to welcoming hand shakes and back slapping. "Sadie, you remind me so much of Mother," he said softly and then he buried his head in her graying hair to hide his tear-filled eyes.

Eventually David realized the family was staring at Lena and Tommy who had finally arrived at the siding. "I'm pleased to introduce my housekeeper, Lena Amacher, and her son, Tommy."

Lena nodded shyly as the visitors acknowledged her presence. The exotic and colorful nature of the entourage almost overwhelmed her.

The first meal with the folks from the West was a testament to Lena's culinary skills. She had insisted that they slaughter a hog as soon as they heard Tallie was coming with his family. They smoked what they could and then Lena spent untold hours in the kitchen making sausage and pickling all the leftovers. David accused her of using the snout, ears, and tail—even the squeal. To his surprise, she didn't disagree, "*Ja,* a *Bernese Platter* is." She was reaching back into her childhood feast days, planning to put up a wall of culinary defense against the visitors. Two days before they were to arrive, she had begun to make *rosti potatoes*, David called them, though she just called them *rosti*. She first had to boil the potatoes and let them sit overnight with a heavy weight on the pan lid. Then she grated them and added a magic combination of milk, butter and salt before she fried the mixture in lots of butter. They were David's favorite.

Upon his arrival, Tallie's Chinese cook was sent to help Lena. Since his vocabulary was apparently limited to "Milky, milky," and he was not really interested in helping this white woman, he was mostly in the way and a constant reminder of the strangeness of the visit. Lottie and her grown children were a real help, though. They always loved coming to the farm and knew how to be useful.

The table was laden with baked chickens, piles of sweet potatoes and the *rosti potatoes*. In the center Lena proudly placed her Swiss specialty, the *Bernese Platter*, which included a fragrant mound of blood and liver sausages, as well as smoked and pickled pork, all neatly arranged on a bed of sauerkraut and beans. There was fresh crusty bread with butter, along with pickles and preserves made from her private recipes. The party finished with three kinds of Lena's *kuchen* made of dried fruit arranged attractively on pastry in a pie tin.

Lena was so busy with the meal preparation that she could not socialize. The opulence of the railroad car itself and the well-dressed ladies and men frightened her. The guests talked in an animated fashion about subjects she could not relate to, with an accent that she could not easily follow. Consequently, Lena was tongue-tied and retreated to the stove whenever possible. She watched from a distance while Tallie and the others spoke of the wonderful changes in Pueblo.

"We plan to explore a new vein at the mine," Seth volunteered. "Prospects look good right now."

Tallie confirmed his statement by saying, "We're hoping to have Arthur open a mining office in Chicago to sell shares." He added, "All these business deals involve the law, and it's hard to find a lawyer who's not shifty or owned by the competition."

It became apparent that they wanted David to leave the farm and join them in the West.

Lena said later that she had never seen David smile and laugh as much as he did during Tallie's visit. The family joked and reminisced with easy laughter around the table, getting louder and more boisterous as they conjured up those happy times of their youth. Finally, Tallie said directly, "David, there's an abundance of opportunity for you in Pueblo. Lawyers are needed to settle land disputes and mineral rights. We need you to advise us on the mines if we are to expand." The table went quiet and all eyes turned to David.

Tallie's wife looked at Lena and said, "I suppose she would have to come, too." David said nothing, but Lena set down the dish she had been passing and found the nerve to respond herself. "I don't suppose I have to go anywhere with anybody unless I want to." David nodded and passed the dish to his right. Carefully avoiding a direct answer to Tallie and any confrontation between Lena and the ladies, he said to the men, "Come, let me show you what we've done to improve the stone barn."

David led Seth, Tallie, and Arthur to the barn where he pointed out the freshly painted louvers, the newly installed hay fork, and the storage facilities that he had built for grain. He regaled them with the weights and prices of beef until he realized that they were not listening. Stepping gingerly around the cow patties, Seth and Tallie were recalling those momentous times almost thirty years ago when the brothers had all worked so hard on Father's barn project. Turning their backs on the barn and David's farming improvements, the "Westerners" returned to the house to finish Lena's *kuchen* and discuss another topic.

Later that evening, relaxed and smoking on the back stoop, Tallie entertained the men with startling tales of the rough and dangerous West. "Big mining interests are watching me closely with a jealous eye," he said. "They threatened to set the mill on fire." Luckily, he was in a position to hold onto the mines in spite of them.

Arthur listened carefully and asked many questions about the mining business. He and Tallie had some long talks out in the stone barn after most of the other folks had gone to bed. Tallie's major concern was that some of the stockholders would want to sell their stock in the mines for less than it had cost them. "The stockholders out west want to see almost immediate return for their investment," he said. Before Arthur left for home, he and Tallie had planned to sell mining shares in Chicago.

The ladies had their own ideas of what was important. "Let's do some sight-seeing," Sadie suggested.

Lottie caught her enthusiasm and proposed, "We'll take a picnic supper to the top of Blue Mounds." She added, "They have a new road now."

They brought the idea to David who had more or less expected to get some fencing done, but he joined in the spirit of the visit. "Perhaps the next day we might take the train into Madison to visit the capitol and university," he said hesitatingly.

Eventually, the marvelous railroad car with its load of bright celebrities coupled on to the next train headed west. It was none too soon for Lena, who was exhausted with meal preparation and the fear that her life would be torn apart.

It had been a wonderful opportunity for David to be with his family once again. However, their invitations to come west had fallen on deaf ears. David could not see leaving the farm. As for practicing law, he had not taken any money for legal services for years. Of course, that did not mean the neighbors did not come to him for advice, and he admitted to himself that he enjoyed helping them now and then. No, he was settled in Wisconsin, and it appeared that Lena was settled as well.

Chapter 16

THE FRAGILITY OF CHILDREN, 1912

The Evans children.

Lena and David developed a comfortable routine. She would cook and clean and tend her garden while David would farm and go to town occasionally to catch up on the latest news. The most sensational gossip centered around Frank Wright, Frank *Lloyd* Wright, some called him. Mr. Wright had helped his aunts over in Wyoming Valley build a dormitory for their school. David was especially interested because Wright's aunts were the Jones sisters who had taught him so well in Spring Green.

Town talk indicated that Frank Wright was going to be moving up here soon, and maybe even build a house. There was lots of chatter about his personal life that David more or less ignored. According to the gossips Wright spent an inordinate amount of time driving around in a big car loaded with ladies dressed in "wrappers." Later on there were some bad feelings because according to the gossips, Wright didn't pay his bills on time, in fact, sometimes not at all. David wondered what his former teachers, Aunt Nell and Aunt Jennie, felt about that.

It was 1912 when a tornado struck the stone barn in the middle of the night. In the morning, David was astonished to discover the barn roof was completely gone. He found most of it sitting in a tumbled heap on top of the hill in the field to the east of the barn. Shingles were scattered all over, but actually there wasn't much other structural damage to the buildings. It was a mess to clean up, and would be a major construction project. David admitted that the roof had been just sitting on top of the walls like a chicken on top of her eggs.

Determined that nothing would remove that roof again, David used iron tie bars to anchor it to the walls and turned to Arthur in Chicago for suggestions about shingles. Arthur recommended a firm that would provide the shingles and put them on for three dollars and fifty cents a square, with a guarantee of five years. The new roof was a good one and lasted a lot longer than five years.

■ ■ ■

Arthur had found some success in Chicago. Mother had been quite proud of his "business qualities," as she called them. The rest of the family felt that she might have been just a little partial to Arthur, her youngest child. Since she disapproved of gambling, it was fortunate that she passed away before he started to wager on the horses. As for David, he wished that Arthur might have stayed with something a bit longer than he did, rather than flitting from one venture to another.

Arthur began as a clerk in the "suit club" business, and before long David began hearing about his real estate deals. He sold stores, rooming houses, and flats. It seemed that Chicago was a hot bed of investment opportunities. Luckily, no one ever heard that he got "burned." At the time David needed help with the barn roof, Arthur had a "swanky office" to sell shares for the brothers' Telluride gold mines called The Jim Crow Gold Mining and Milling Co. and The Junta Gold Mining and Milling Co. Arthur wrote in May of 1912, "I secured an office in one of the best office buildings on LaSalle Street and we are going to go into it in a first class shape as you can see by the letterhead, and we will have an even better letterhead next time if we make a go out of it."

Tallie was visiting Arthur in Chicago two months later when he received a telegraph from Seth announcing that the large mill they had leased for ten years had burned to the ground. Tallie believed that it was probably set afire by the "big mining interests." Arthur reported that Tallie was "… in a position to hold the mines in spite of them (the big mining interests) … because he had a small mill in which he can operate about fourteen tons or about $120 a day…."

Another of Arthur's letters quoted an old Welshman who knew mining. He said Tallie's business, "…showed up better than any mining proposition that I ever saw." No matter how persuasive Arthur and Tallie's letters, David refrained from investing in the mine shares. He saw mining as a risky business, especially in Telluride, Colorado.

Tallie had intended to visit David on his way back home, but he was notified of bad news by another telegraph. It appeared that his daughter was dying. The little girl had taken sick with typhoid caused by drinking the river water in Pueblo. Pneumonia set in, and she could not fight them both. The child died while Tallie was on the train heading home.

Some months later Arthur wrote David of more bad luck, "We are not able to do anything with Tallie's mining stock. Between the two of us we spent about $200 in advertising and did not get any results from it, and we think that we could go ahead and spend more money with the same results." David learned later that Arthur had to give up his fancy office.

■ ■ ■

Tallie wasn't the only one to lose a child that year. Lena's baby had grown into a fine little boy, quiet and quick-witted. Like his mother, he was a determined little piece. As soon as he could walk, Tommy followed David around the house and yard like a shadow. David could see that Tommy wanted to learn and help, and he found great pleasure teaching him to do chores. David would often take Tommy to the barn and bounce him around in the hay a bit after dinner. Watching him play and try to help was a delicious pleasure David relished each day.

It was mid-February when Tommy fell ill. At first, Lena passed it off as a little cold. After a day of fever, David had the doctor come by. The doctor applied leech after leech in the accepted practice of bleeding to reduce a fever. Lena could not watch what she considered a travesty worked upon her little lamb. David counted as the doctor pulled off ten of the blood filled slugs. Shaking his head, the doctor packed up the monsters. "It's pneumonia. He's in the hands of the Lord now."

The fever continued to rage, and Tommy's frail body could not fight it. Early in the morning of the 23rd, Lena called to David, "You need to come now. Wash up and come to Tommy's room." David found Lena sitting on Tommy's bed. She held his hands as if she would never let them go. He was coughing a bit. Then he gasped and lay there quietly. Finally, the shallow breaths ceased, and David's little shadow was gone.

They buried Tommy in the White Church Cemetery. Some folks might say the stone was too big at two and a half feet. It was taller than Tommy had been, but it gave Lena some comfort. When asked what to put on the stone, David and Lena couldn't answer. Their hearts were too full. They decided on, "At rest."

When spring finally came that year, David bought a small herd of Brown Swiss springing heifers. He had planned to remodel the first floor of the barn into a commercial dairy operation by adding stanchions. This seemed as good a time as any. He liked the looks of the herd, and he rather hoped they would remind Lena of Switzerland. She might leave off crying and cheer up a bit. David admitted to himself that he missed the spring in her step as much as he missed the little boy. "Do you think these might do?" he asked Lena as he and the hired man drove in the herd of eight bred cows. "Can you help us with them?"

"Ja, ja is a good herd," she spoke authoritatively as she examined their flanks and udders, then she turned to David. "I'll be liking these."

They had calves just after the spring rains. Lena knew what to do without any direction. She made sure the newborns were up and sucking as soon as they were cleaned. David even found her helpful in turning a calf that was coming back feet first. He caught her smiling at the antics of the little calves and looked forward to seeing the lively housekeeper he had become accustomed to.

One night as she was serving up some boiled ham, Lena asked if David was going to make cheese. He had not given it a thought until recently.

David had inherited part ownership of the local cheese factory. The factory contracted with farmers in a two or three-mile radius and thus had an adequate supply of milk to make cheese profitably. David nodded to Lena and puffed contentedly on his pipe. As usual, she was way ahead of him.

Chapter 17

FROM HOUSEKEEPER
TO BRIDE, 1914

Lena.

It was unbearably warm that summer. Indeed, it turned out to be one of those years that everyone remembers for Nature's excesses. David found himself speaking harshly with the hired men and kicking the dog just because he happened to be there. Churchgoers spent a lot of time on their knees asking for respite and forgiveness. Married men debated the weather prospects with their wives and everyone else who would listen. David scanned the heavens for likely rain clouds.

It was downright painful to walk to the barn and hear the grass crunch with every step. It was even more difficult to watch the cattle. They still looked to be the best beef herd east of the Mississippi, but it seemed their coats had lost their luster in the dust. Frequently after milking, Lena reported, "another cow be dried up now."

It was July, and instead of the lush green grass the cattle needed to put weight on, the pastures were yellow in the blazing sun of ninety-plus to one hundred degrees. At night there seemed no life at all. Indeed, there was a stillness when the sun set and the wind stopped that boded no good for the farmer.

Early one morning David set out by way of Trout Creek to replenish the salt blocks at the Spring Green pasture. From a distance the little creek looked like an oasis of verdant greens and gold. Once there, the swift little current was too much to resist. He pulled off his sweaty socks and wading in. My God, it was great! It was not very deep and the smooth stones on the bottom made it wonderful for wading. The coolness was startling, blessedly relaxing and comforting. First he sat on the bank and watched his feet float up to the surface. The water held him in a spell as he pulled off his shirt. Then, looking around at the silent willows, he pulled off his trousers. In a delirious moment of peace and relief, he knelt to splash water all over himself. The sun smiled down on his antics, and he shut his eyes briefly to relish the blessed coolness that restored his body and spirit.

David could hardly admit to himself that he had waded in his underwear. He had just planned to cool off his feet. Luckily, there was no one to see an old bachelor like him taking a dip. He felt a bit foolish, wet clothes and all, but those cows did not mind him a bit, and the prospects of a full-scale drought seemed far away after splashing in the creek.

There was more cover at the Spring Green pasture, and the cattle looked perkier than at home. He did notice that some of the bushes near the "crick" were a bit ragged, reminding him of the stories told by old timers who held that cows will eat leaves from trees and bushes if need be.

On the ride back to the house, he almost went for another splash, but passed by because he figured that he would have a fine time explaining wet clothes to the hired men when he arrived home.

It was quiet when he returned. The men were working in the shade of the horse barn mending harness and whatever. No one seemed to have much ambition, and after his dip, he did not have the heart to stir them to greater activity. "It's not as bad up Spring Green way," he offered. "I do believe we're just running through a mighty long dry spell here."

So many of the milk cows had dried up in the past weeks, it would not take but a couple of the hands to complete chores and do the milking. "Why don't you bachelors finish here and let the family men go home?" David suggested, turning away from the eternal grumbling that came from one man or another no matter what he said.

There was a cold supper on the table when he came in from the barn. The thinly sliced beef tongue and a mound of potato salad had been carefully covered by a perfectly ironed and creased napkin. There was fresh bread and butter as well as a dish of shining peaches. It should have contented him, but it didn't.

It was foolishness to iron linen and then put it over food, and to open a can of peaches. Did Lena think the grocery money he gave her grew on some bush in the side yard? David wondered. And furthermore, where was she? Not much for gallivanting, she was usually around the house somewhere cleaning or fixing or doing something in the garden. She never did fancy needlework, on account of her eyes, he presumed.

He just was not accustomed to having her gone. David served himself water with a dipper from the bucket standing by the sink and slowly went to his place at the table. As he ate supper and savored the slippery coolness of the peaches, he looked over at her chair. He could not remember when she started to sit down with him to eat supper. There just did not seem to be much reason for her eating on her feet with him sitting. He forgot if it was she or he who mentioned it first. It might have been Lena. She was not one to set matters aside and try to come in the back door sideways.

When he found out where she had disappeared to that night, he forgave her directly. But, now he was perturbed, annoyed you could say. He just felt that she should have been at home.

As usual he gathered his account book, the almanac, and yesterday's Barneveld paper that one of the men had brought over in the morning, and settled down on the stoop. He was more or less expecting Lena to come and find him, and then he would see what she had been up to.

He studied the paper trying to eke out any hints of weather and markets. It seemed pointless tonight. His cousin Sadie Evans read tea leaves, but he saw little reason in studying them, either. If the dry spell became a drought, they would have to sell cattle. It was impossible to keep a herd of over four hundred fed after the pastures dried up. If they cut two hundred of the old cows, would that be enough? And then would the fences hold when the pastures gave out? The almanac was no help, and that woman still was not back where she ought to be.

The clock struck nine o'clock, and David moved slowly upstairs to his room, but he had not shut and locked the house door as usual. That would be too mean-spirited, and he and Lena could have words over a good breakfast. Each step up the stairs carried him into the oven-like heat of the second floor. Usually he enjoyed some kind of cross ventilation, but tonight there was no air at all. As soon as he lay down, he fell to sleep. Then he awoke. When, he was not too sure. He had not heard the clock, and he could not see the moon from his bedroom window. He was unbearably warm—hot and restless with what he didn't want to acknowledge as worry. The sheet was soaked with sweat. There was no way he could sleep any more.

Like those hot nights long ago when his brothers were home, he decided to drag a quilt out to the stone barn where he would curl up close to the rock walls and try to settle down.

However, David was to sleep little that night. Moving quietly so as not to wake Lena, if she had returned, he crept down the stairs, where he looked into the open door of her room and observed that her bed was still made up properly. He opened the house door and paused on the stoop. The almost full moon was watching his every move. It was still and quiet, though he felt that the leaves on the trees rustled slightly. What a blessing if a breeze came up. He moved slowly, quietly, to the shadow of the stone barn where the moon could not see him.

As he turned to spread his quilt, he noticed a movement in the darkness. He could see a form in white moving off the porch. At first he failed to identify what he was seeing. He watched the graceful figure move slowly down the steps where it paused. Then he knew it was part of a poem he had once memorized for the Jones sisters:

It was an apparition of delight
dressed in the darkness of the night

The apparition went into the side yard where Lena had planted a few flowers, "To remind me of home," she had said. Transfixed, he watched the figure move among the flowers. It appeared to be leaning toward them, perhaps to smell their day-dried fragrance in the relative coolness of the night or to whisper encouragement to them at this dreadful time.

Dressed in the darkness of the night, the woman moved back to the stoop, sat down and began brushing her hair. She brushed carefully, as if each stroke were a pleasure, and without realizing it, David began counting the strokes. She stood up and continued brushing, and he could see sparks as the brush left her hair hanging lightly in the air. Then the counting of her strokes did not seem to matter any more as he moved carefully forward.

The woman looked up just as he came into the moonlight, and she did not seem surprised to see him. David had to shake himself as he recognized Lena for herself and realized that she was staring at him like a startled colt, without her steel rimmed glasses. Her lovely face fairly glowed in the light of the moon, while her hair framed her head like charged ebony. She moved toward him as the breeze picked up, and her figure was softly outlined against the sky.

■ ■ ■

David never looked at Lena the same after that night. Perhaps it was a spell that she or the moon cast over them both. Certainly it was a good spell, and they never did have that little talk about where she had been and what she had been doing. Furthermore, some clouds finally came in the end of the week, and they had a regular "goose-downer" on Sunday. The drought was broken for sure.

The harvesting chores kept them both very busy. There was no end to the preserving that Lena did that fall. If David needed her, he could find her working over a hot stove canning tomatoes, beets, and green beans. It was like he was really seeing her for the first time in all those years that she had been his housekeeper.

That fall David found that the grain binder worked well, and they soon had a good bin of oats for the horses. The stone barn was full of hay, and the hired men were promising that they would have more bushels of corn than last year. As David brought in the last load of corn each day, he looked forward to washing up and learning what Lena had prepared for their dinner. More than that, he anticipated seeing her and telling her about their progress and trials in the fields, and he delighted in her little stories about household activities.

To the surprise of just about everyone, David and Lena married that December. One amazingly clear winter day, they hitched up the wagon and headed for Dodgeville, not telling anybody their business. Judge Aldo Jenks married them, and afterward they had a proper wedding lunch at the hotel.

On the way back to the farm, David had Lena pick out some good-looking fabric at the dressmaker's, and she tried on some hats to match. It was not until the next day that the hired men figured out what had happened.

■ ■ ■

That first year of married life was a busy one for both of them. The dairy herd was growing, and David found himself depending more and more on Lena to help with the milking, as well as with a lot of other things. He enjoyed the evenings when she would ask him about what was in the newspaper. He would read what he thought would interest her, and then he would read about things that interested him. She enjoyed them all and usually had something to say about each one. They never talked about Tommy, although they both missed him terribly.

■ ■ ■

It was late fall of the following year when he noticed a change in Lena. Even with the extra chores, she appeared to be gaining weight. She was thirty-two. Maybe that happened to women at that time of life. He believed that it was not his business to be commenting on such a thing to a woman, and let it go.

The Evans girls finally brought him up short when they announced, "Congratulations Cousin David, you're going to be a father."

He confessed to being excited and proud, and curious as well, wondering just what kind of a child they would have together.

When Lena's time came, he sent the hired man to the Evans' house where there was a phone to call Doctor Hamilton in Ridgeway. Then the girls called down to Amacher Hollow and packed up the sled to fetch Lena's sister, Ida. It was slow going, for the sky had just cleared after a fresh snow. There was no rushing the horses.

When the girls finally returned with Ida and began steaming around the house, they told David that he was not needed. Dr. Hamilton drove up and became rather busy himself. It was a hard thing to hear he couldn't help, but finding his legs a bit wobbly, he sat down at the kitchen table. He decided the coffee tasted good with a bit of brandy, and then he tried to say a prayer.

Their little girl was born early the next morning. After what seemed a very long time with Ida and the Evans girls running in and out of the kitchen carrying hot water and dirty linen, Dr. Hamilton announced that David could come into the bedroom. David walked through the front parlor to their downstairs bedroom where a fresh clean smell reached him as he opened the door.

Lena lay with her hair brushed out around her face. Her smile was tender as she looked down at the tiny, mewing creature in her arms and then into her husband's face.

"Our daughter," David said, and reached awkwardly for the little bundle.

"Her name is Margarette," Lena said. Then he looked from one beautiful face to the other and knew himself to be the luckiest man alive.

Chapter 18

LENA

The Thomas family after Walter's birth.

David believed Lena was a prize, a pearl of great worth. He pondered her all his life. It seemed that the older he became, the younger and stronger she grew, even after three children. She never contradicted him, and they never argued, but he found himself listening to her and wanting to do things to make life easier for her. Just the same, he knew that he was making the important decisions. She helped with the chores like a man, but she also did things, womanly things, that made him stop and think.

Lena taught Margarette to embroider. She did it just by feel. He could hardly believe the little girl's work and her mother's patience. Margarette also learned from her mother how to knit mittens, and every day Lena would read "Uncle Wiggley" from the newspaper, never missing a story.

Their little girl was always looking for the rascally Uncle Wiggley near the old wood pile. One day soon after she had turned four, Margarette wiggled around in the brush pile and finally caught him, the rabbit she believed was Uncle Wiggley. She brought the squirming bunny to the house. "I've got him," she called. "It's Uncle Wiggley for sure."

"Put that animal down," Lena ordered in surprised amazement. Margarette did as she was told, and Uncle Wiggley scampered back to the brush pile. Of course Margarette was crushed. Her mother and father had a difficult time convincing her that the rabbit would be happier under the brush pile than clutched in her chubby arms.

Tucked away in the corner of the kitchen was a little rocking chair that Lena would use when she wanted to "set a minute" after putting something in the oven. Sometimes she would be doing a bit of knitting and sometimes just sitting, rocking and resting her eyes. In all their years together David had never asked about her eyes. He learned about them late in their married life.

■ ■ ■

One day David and the men finished their fence repairs early. David planned to surprise Lena by coming home mid-afternoon. When he arrived at the kitchen door, Lena was nursing baby Harold, and Walter was sitting bolt upright on the floor staring at his mother. Margarette was holding Lena's glasses, alternately putting them on, trying to see through them, and taking them off.

Lena was telling a story. It was about a little girl in Switzerland who was not much older than Margarette. David paused and listened. "She had come home from school hot and feverish. The little girl lay in bed with the measles for two weeks. She began to have bad dreams at night because each day she awoke, the world was darker than the day before."

Margarette handed her mother the heavy glasses. "What was the little girl's name?" she asked. "Was it Lena? Was it you, Mother?"

David could see Lena nodding her head, smiling. She went on. "My mother collected little poppies that grew wild—mallow, your father says. They had little round fruits, we called them 'cheeses,' and she would cook them up, leaves and everything, and put poultices on my eyes." And then Lena paused for effect. "After a few days it was light again, and I could see."

"But why do you wear glasses?" Margarette asked. Lena reached for her glasses and adjusted them on her face, looking up to smile at David's shadowy figure in the doorway.

Lena continued her story, "One wonderful day we went to the big city. Mother dressed me in my best frock, and Father drove us to the eye doctor's office. Father was very quiet and uncomfortable in the city, but I believe that he was also brave and determined. Knocking boldly on the doctor's door, he announced to the woman who opened it, 'We have come for a pair of spectacles.'

I looked at the blurry figure in the door way and said, 'Please, I want to be going back to school.' The woman led us directly to the kind doctor who tried many lenses on each eye until he finally found ones that made my world clearer."

"Only with these on," Lena said, looking at the three children and David arranged so solemnly in front of her, "can I see my precious ones."

■ ■ ■

David was always learning things about Lena. He had failed to realize when he married her, that he would receive her family in the bargain. It was just natural for the Amachers to want to be together, so even though they socialized throughout the year, they had an annual picnic. One Sunday, late in summer, David and Lena would finish early milking and load up the wagon for the trip to the Amacher family home near Arena. Later on, David's cousin, Jack Evans, would take the family in his Nash. In those days the roads had no gravel. They were all mud or dust, depending on the weather. Jack was a fine driver, who never worried, and never got excited. He just headed that old car with its big wheels in the right direction and drove. They could have gotten stuck anywhere, but never did.

At first David felt strange at these gatherings. He would just sit quietly and eat, listening. The family reminiscences stretched back to their life in Switzerland where Lena was born in 1883 and enjoyed a "Heidi" childhood until she was partially blinded by the measles. He could tell that Lena had loved her life in the mountains. The family never forgot those Alps. Even

David could close his eyes and see the mountains. He believed that the Alps could not have been much different than the majestic and mighty mountains of the American West.

In that old country of awesome beauty, children had important responsibilities. One of the most exciting and important times of Lena's youth was preparing to go to the mountains with the goats every spring. Her father would go ahead to clean the mountain hut and set up for making cheese. He loaded a wooden frame strapped onto his back with a heavy kettle for the cheese and set off the day before his family left. Cheese-making provided a good part of the family income.

The goats had been sheltered for the winter in a shed attached to the family's living quarters. They were quivering to get out and run in the spring sunshine where they could enjoy the tender shoots of new grass. Lena remembered one spring in particular. Her mother loaded a pack on her back with loaves of bread. "Watch out for your little brothers now," she admonished her daughter. Leading goats, carrying loaves of bread, minding her siblings, it was quite a job for a little girl. The goats were giddy in the spring air, and her brothers adventurous. Lena lost a loaf of bread by the time she reached the shelter at the top of the mountain, and her mother scolded her until she broke into tears.

■ ■ ■

After Lena finished school, she went to work at a fireworks factory which shipped most of their wares to America. It was hard for David to imagine a partially blind girl making firecrackers, but the job didn't last long. There was an explosion at the factory, and Lena found herself out of a job. Then she began paying more attention to the letters from her brothers, Chris and Peter, who were the first members of the Amacher family to leave for America. It didn't take her long to make up her mind, and Lena left next with her older brothers, Alfred, Fred, and John.

Her brothers had settled first on land close to New Glarus, Wisconsin, before discovering an area near Arena, which became known as Amacher Hollow. The valley had high hills on both sides and reminded them of home. The boys wrote of good farmland, opportunity, and growing cities. Ultimately, Lena's parents, as well as her sisters, Ida and Helen, were persuaded that the boys had found a good home place, and they made the trip from Switzerland to Wisconsin. Sisters Mary Ann and Rosa remained in Switzerland with their husbands and families.

After an Amacher picnic, there was always music with singing, dancing, and yodeling. Lena knew that David was very much against dancing, and card playing. She could dance and sing like a sweet bird, and she yodeled in a haunting fashion that David confessed to enjoying. He maintained the Good Lord couldn't object to it either. However, there was no other way for his wife; she had to give up her dancing. Lena would sit and watch and listen to the music, her foot tapping and her face eager. He liked the lively music as well, for he had learned to jig out west as a young man. Dancing a jig seemed like a safe thing to do since he had no need of a partner.

Besides the annual picnic in Amacher Hollow, there was no end of visiting. The Evans sisters across the hill at the next farm were often at the farm, and Lena would frequently walk over to the Evans' house, to "get the kinks out." Occasionally, Aunt Helen came out from Madison to visit for a few days. They saw a lot of Aunt Ida, too, especially after she married Dave Baumgartner, who made cheese near the Hollow.

Sometimes Lena would take the wagon to visit her relatives. She loved to tell of the time she tipped over on the road to Arena. Margarette went with her often, but this time the child had stayed at home. Lena must have not been paying attention, for she ran into a little white marker post on the edge of the road. Luckily, she was unhurt, though the wagon needed some repair. Perhaps even she forgot that she didn't see well. After that, one of the children would always ride over with her when their chores were finished.

■ ■ ■

Lena never failed to have a fine meal on the table for the family and the three or four hired men who ate three meals a day with them every day of the week. Only occasionally would the family ask for dessert and find there was nothing. Then they would hear Lena give good reasons or a small rebuke. "I've been dosing those calves with the scours since five o'clock in the morning," she would say, or she would look at the children and comment, "Strange, there is usually a big pile of wood by the stove when I go to cook. I couldn't find any wood today except outside on the woodpile, and it took me a long time to haul it in for supper."

Every fall she made a family event of ordering fruit from the *Sears Roebuck Catalog*. The children could pick out their favorites. The orchard provided plenty of apples, so they usually chose plums and pears. Lena selected currents, raisins, citron, and prunes for the Swiss Pear Bread she made for *Weihnachts* or Christmas, then they all spent time looking over the other items in the "wish book."

Margarette ignored the beautifully dressed dolls. "Father," she said, pointing to the drawing of a sled. "It's a Flyer. May I have one?" she asked hopefully. Her brothers looked from Father to Margarette, hoping he would say yes.

David just shook his head. "We need a new roof on the shed," he commented as if that explained everything. Sometimes there was enough money for extras, but usually the order didn't include much besides food. Even so David still felt like Santa Claus when he brought the packages from the depot. The first time they received an order, he remembered thinking that he had never seen so much food in his life, outside a town store.

Mostly David stayed out of the kitchen except to eat, but he especially enjoyed the smell of Lena's bread. The twelve to fourteen loaves were baked at one time on a big tray that just fit into their wood burning stove. After her sister Ida gave her a special little iron, she made *Hairdovvel* and *Braetzli*, tasty crisp cookies impressed with a design made by the flat iron.

Lena was a member of the Swiss Evangelical Church in Barneveld, and an active member of the Ladies' Aid Society which held annual suppers and other money raisers where they enjoyed her delicious baked goods. There was no telling how many cookies and cakes she made for her church.

Threshing time was really an exciting and challenging time for everyone. It was thrilling to hear the steam engine thundering down the road. From a distance it sounded like a clumsy giant clanking and clanging its way to the farm. The neighbors and the thresher would come in time to begin work just after the dew was off the wheat or oats.

Lena began baking a big batch of drop cookies at least three days ahead of the men. She would make up her pie crusts and then set a big ham to boil. The day before the thresher arrived, she baked a full batch of fourteen loaves of bread. The night before, she peeled potatoes, estimating about four potatoes per man.

Ida and Helen always came to help with the cooking. Everyone especially enjoyed Helen's delicious lemon pies and other desserts. The womenfolk prepared cabbage salad and selected tomatoes for slicing. They dressed and prepared chickens almost nonstop for at least three days. It took all this to be ready to feed upwards of twenty workers and their families for sometimes three to four meals.

Lena's special challenge was to get the thirty cows milked and guess correctly when the men would be home from the field so the dinner would be ready and hot. She gained a little time by insisting that they all wash up on in the basins on the porch. Some of the neighbors grumbled, but they washed up and felt better for it. When Margarette was old enough, she was the "waitress," shuttling food from stove to table, pouring milk, and cutting desserts.

They cooked with lard in those days, butchering a pig in the fall, and sometimes in the spring. The men would do this right on the farm, smoking the hams and sending the rest of the meat to the kitchen to be prepared for canning or frying. Lena would fry up the ham slices and layer them with grease in a huge crock which they stored in the cool basement. The rich, succulent pork tasted delicious on bitter cold winter nights. The butcher in town cut up their beef, which they brought home in the wagon to be canned.

As soon as the first robins were sighted, Lena announced, "Ja, Jaass, yes! It's time for to move the stove." David came to learn that there was a lot more to that statement than just he and the hired man using two notched sticks to pick up the stove and carry it out to the kitchen shanty below the house.

It meant water, pails and pails of water, for days. He had come to learn that Lena was indeed a very clean lady, and when it came to spring cleaning, she outdid herself. Margarette worked right along with her mother, scrubbing everything. The white chairs used in the kitchen fairly sparkled when Lena finished washing them. All the bedding was removed from the beds and washed, the mattresses aired on the lawn, and the bed frames scrubbed. By nightfall, the beds were always made and back in place, clean and sweet smelling.

The water for cleaning and washing clothes was heated in a copper boiler. In the summer it was almost pleasant to work outside. Lena would show Margarette how to scrub the men's overalls on a bench. "They're too heavy for me," Margarette complained.

"Let me help you," her mother suggested. Together they would rinse and twist the clothes to get the water out, then peg them on the line for the wind and sun to dry.

It was Lena's job to round up the cows for milking twice a day. She never missed a morning or evening. It seemed as if she had an internal alarm clock that told her those cows needed her at 4:00 a.m. She never let anyone else touch the milking equipment. She used lye for cleaning, and of course, did everything by hand. The Thomases never had any problems with the inspectors. As a matter of fact, one inspector said to David, "Your wife has the cleanest milk house in three counties." They milked thirty head, more or less, twice a day, and when the children became old enough, they took over the chore of hauling the milk to the cheese factory down on what they now call Route Eighteen.

Lena worked alongside David, never mind all the cooking and housecleaning that she also did. Not one hired man could match her for dealing with calving or milking, and she never shrank from hard work except for one morning that David remembered clearly to his chagrin.

Lena's sister Ida was visiting. Margarette was attending school in Madison, and her brothers were busy with their own chores. David had slept poorly and was feeling out of sorts. Lena told him, "I have a terrible headache. Ida will milk the cows."

David shook his head, motioning her to get up. "If you can't do it, then we may as well quit farming," he said. He knew he couldn't go on without her help.

Chapter 19

MARGARETTE

Margarette with her two brothers, Walter and Baby Harold.

Margarette was born in 1916, Walter came along four years later, and then Harold was born in 1922. David was fifty-six when he and Lena started having children. He needed good help on the farm, so it was natural for him to look forward to the time when they could depend on their own family for help. Luckily, it was not long before Margarette could split wood as well as any hired hand, and the good thing was that she seemed to like working with her father.

Sometimes work was not too different from play. Her father was a fast runner, and just for fun he would race Margarette to the hay field. Eventually, Margarette could run like a deer, and beat her father most of the time.

David and Lena kept Margarette home until she was almost nine. They believed there wasn't much use sending children to school when they were too young. Lena taught her numbers and letters, and David taught Margarette to read using the newspaper and books.

David depended on Margarette's help and companionship. Often she would "ride along" to open gates and run errands. "Daddy, Daddy," she called when she saw him harnessing the horses for a trip to the mill, "Mother said I can come with you and help."

It was a fine day, and she enjoyed playing in the mill stream while her father arranged to pay for the lumber and loaded it up. On the way home, David told her stories of when he was about her age and living near the mill. She entertained him by singing little songs that Lena had taught her.

When they came to their yard gate, Margarette bounded off the wagon to open it, "I'll get the gate, Daddy," she said as she jumped onto the road.

David pulled the horses up, "Whoa! Whoa, I say." The team fought the reins, and in a horrible fraction of a second, one of the horses raised his foot and kicked Margarette in the side of the head. David struggled to control the horses and keep them away from her frail body.

The only sounds he heard from Margarette were small and muffled, like that of an injured animal. Then, as he climbed down from the wagon seat, two burly fellows from Barneveld ran up. They had been cutting weeds nearby and had seen the horses rear. It was Tom Lewis who picked Margarette up and rushed her into the house. Lena was horrified, for her little girl was unconscious. "What happened? She's bleeding—"

After they saw Margarette safely to her own bed, the two fellows unloaded the wagon, and David headed back to Ridgeway for Dr. Hedges. When the doctor finally arrived, he was relieved to find her alert. He looked Margarette over and said, "We'll need to shave her head to see her wounds more clearly."

"Oh no, I don't want to be bald!" she wailed. Margarette was so distressed by the shaving process that it was hard to say why she had a headache—from the fall or the loss of her hair. Lena cleaned her face tenderly and continued applying cold compresses until the child's breathing became steady and she slept. Happily for them, Margarette perked right up after the swelling went down and her headache went away.

David was proud that the accident never prevented Margarette from enjoying horses. The only thing she struggled with was putting on their big collars. With the assistance of her older cousins, Margarette even tried to break horses. Always the leader, she lined up three of her cousins explaining, "Today we will break Dad's new horse. We'll do it together."

Margarette held the reins tightly, getting on first. The other three mounted behind her on the horse's broad, bare back. For a brief moment the horse didn't move. Then, rearing up with great disdain, he dumped them one by one on the ground.

David arrived just in time to watch them land in a tumbled heap, laughing hysterically. Luckily, the horse trotted off and waited for a more dignified training program. Thankful that no one had been hurt, David said, "That's enough now, we'll let the hired man give him a try this afternoon."

Margarette's own horse was a bronco she named Old Pet. She had lots of tricks up her sleeve and would occasionally stop on a dime, letting Margarette slide to the ground. Thomases always had six horses or so. Luckily none of the children ever had a broken bone.

If there was excitement, Margarette liked to be in the center of it. Once when she was four or five, she and her mother were visiting the neighbors where they stopped to admire some geese. Without any warning, the big birds attacked the little girl, hissing and flapping their wings. Margarette was so scared that she jumped right up on her mother's shoulders. From that vantage point, she stifled a sob and asked, "Are these wild geese, Mother?"

On the home place, Lena had always been good at raising chickens and ducks, as well as few geese. One year she wanted to try guinea hens.

"They look nice," she said when David asked what good they were. When she ordered the Rhode Island Red chicks that year, she did order a few Guineas, and David did not see any harm in them.

However, he had occasion to change his mind one morning when he took delivery of a load of lumber. The noisy guinea hens darted out in front of the delivery wagon horses, squawking like a fox was after them.

The delivery man, who was still in the wagon, looked up just in time to see the horses bolt and run. He dropped down behind the buckboard, pulling back on the reins. Margarette and Lena, drawn to the door by the ruckus, watched as the horses went around in the barnyard. Finally, they went through a board fence and hung up the wagon. "Perhaps we don't need the nice-looking guineas any more," David suggested to Lena as he surveyed the scene.

Lena nodded sadly, "They were such pretty little things. Too bad they couldn't keep quiet."

■ ■ ■

Continuing to look for more adventure Margarette bragged, "I can go the whole length of the stone barn."

"Bet you a nickel you can't," Walter taunted.

"Just you watch," she said as she climbed the hay bales at one end of the barn and jumped up to grab the hay fork track. Her brother fell silent as he watched her go hand-over-hand from one end of the barn to the other. If there had been no hay to break a fall, she could have broken her neck.

Walter told on her. David believed he would put an end to such dangerous foolishness. "We'll have no more circus acrobatics," he said. "I'll see that the men put some ropes up so you children can swing on them safely." Even today there are still ropes hanging in the stone barn, and whenever children come, they go to the barn for rope swinging and jumping into the hay.

Margarette was strong and very handy when it came time to make hay. First she learned to drive the dump rake around the field collecting all the loose hay after cutting. Always game for a new challenge, Margarette also learned to drive the hay wagon. Only once did she let the horse get too close to the fence and shattered the wagon tongue. Her father gave her the "Dickens," but could not bring himself to punish her.

It is a tricky job to drive a hay wagon on Wisconsin hills, and Margarette didn't like to waste time. She moved the horses right along. One day her luck ran out, and she tipped the wagon over, dumping an entire load of loose hay. There was nothing else to do but right the wagon and pitch it back in. Her father could see how angry she was, but she pitched hay right along with the hired hands. At supper that night he teased, "So Margarette, you're getting to be a wild driver, are you?"

She began to answer with anger when her father reached over and patted her hand. "The horses were really frisky," she said and gave her father a very small smile.

In spring Margarette loved to run barefoot, squashing the mud and manure between her toes. When she was not running, she was bareback on Old Pet racing 'round and 'round the house driving her mother out of her mind. One day, her father needed Margarette's help, and she was nowhere to be found.

Lena did not seem worried, and when Margarette arrived home late in the afternoon laden with two brimming milk pails of juicy blackcaps, her father couldn't scold her too much. Lena made pies and jam from the berries, and Margarette was a great help to David the next day.

An excellent teacher, Lena realized her daughter's active mind needed more challenges. "Margarette's smart and growing up fast," she said.

"You might be right, but I do believe she will catch up with her classmates very quickly." David said. Margarette was almost nine when she began to attend elementary school in Jennieton.

She often walked to school with Bertha Lewis who was her teacher. Many times Allen Massey and the Arneson children, Ollie and Niome, as well as Ted Thompson's children, joined her.

Only occasionally would she walk with the Strutt girls who lived over the hill to the north of Jennieton School. They were great teases. "It's best to splash cold water on your face to ward off the cold," they advised the little girl. She did it once, and it was very cold. Margarette hid her face in her scarf when the girls laughed cruelly at her plight.

When the students finally arrived at the schoolhouse in winter, they had to start the fire. After the students were warm enough, the teacher put a tin pan of water on the stove. In it each child placed his or her jar of soup so that by lunchtime, the meal was hot and comforting. After lunch, students as well as the teacher kept warm outside with fox-and-geese and snowball fights.

Margarette loved sports and did her share of sleigh riding in the winter. The students played as long as the teacher allowed, while taking turns to use the frigid outhouse before going back into the warmth of the fire and reading lessons. When the warm weather came, Margarette learned to play softball with a big fat kitten ball during recess. She excelled in softball, and never missed playing games between other schools. She gladly did her chores before or after the games. Margarette loved her friends and teachers, especially Mable Kurth and Hazel Cretney. She was as good in school as her parents expected.

She never stopped running. At home she raced her brothers and cousins, even trying hurdles. Often she was the winner. Eager for more competition, the children often raced the train. They heard it coming from a distance, blowing its whistle at each crossing starting from Ridgeway or Barneveld. "I'll race you to the trestle," Margarette shouted to anyone who might take up her challenge.

"Last one there is a 'monkey's uncle,'" was the usual response. The children had plenty of time to run up to the railroad trestle in their back pasture, just north of what is now Highway 18/151. They would wave and shout to the engineer. He always waved back.

■ ■ ■

Margarette came home from school one spring day to discover that her father had decided to make a big change in the stone barn. Lena and David had talked about it off and on for years, and David finally made the decision even though it meant changing his father's barn. "We need to modernize," David said. "My father was forward thinking when he built the barn, and we need to keep up the family tradition."

Walter had built the lower barn for horses. David and Lena had been milking there for years, and the doors were too narrow for the equipment. David was bone tired of mucking out the barn by hand and hauling manure in a wheel barrow. At dinner he announced his plans. "I hired a stone mason to help me with the job so we can do it right and not jeopardize the stability of the barn."

Lena put down the dish of creamed corn she was bringing to the table and began, "What about the arches—"

David responded, "We are modernizing," and that was the end of the discussion.

The men began the job the next day and had made some good progress when David looked up. There was Lena, her hands on Margarette's shoulders, watching. Mother and daughter were silent, but they looked as if they were watching a family member receive an amputation. Marveling at the sentimentality of womankind, David continued his work. When the men were finished, the arch over the opening was almost unchanged, and they could finally get equipment in and out.

Like all farm children, Margarette continued to do her chores when she started school. These included helping her mother round up the cows for milking. It meant jumping on her little pony at 4:00 a.m. One morning she and her father remember with regret. Margarette said that she felt ill, and Lena wanted her to stay in bed.

"Stay in bed when there are chores to do?" David could not believe her impudence. "Tarnation, Margarette!" he shouted up the stairs, "Get up or otherwise you're going to have to leave." She was shocked by his tone. She got up, dressed, and left the house to bring in the cows. Her father realized then how desperately he needed her help on the farm. He was getting close to seventy years old. The boys were too young to be of much use.

■ ■ ■

In no time at all, Margarette was walking a mile and a half to the high school in Barneveld. Thin and strong, she strode along in sturdy shoes and black stockings, and she donned buckle rubber boots in the winter.

The first day of school after Christmas break, Margarette wore a new dress that Lena's sister had made. She looked good in it, and very grown-up. At dinner that night she reported, "My classmates admired my dress," she began. "They say that the Thomas girl and the Evanses are the best-dressed young ladies in the county."

"Another one said that my father's very rich," Margarette continued. "They said Father has 1,000 acres."

"And how did you respond to these girls," Lena asked.

I told them, "I never saw any money, but we are rich in land," Margarette said. Lena and David were proud of their daughter's reply.

The farm was profitable that year, and Lena had been promoting modern conveniences for some time now.

"I don't have any need for electricity in the house. It's for city folks, and don't tell me I'm getting too old to go to an outhouse," David grumbled. After the flush toilet was installed, he was proud that he had given in to Lena.

It was 1937. Margarette had received a special assignment in her senior year of high school. It was to write a biography. She chose to write about her father, and she interviewed him just like a city journalist.

"When were you born?" She asked her father. "Where did you teach school? Where did you learn to be a lawyer? What did you do out West?"

She received satisfactory answers to all her questions but the last, "Why did you come back home to the farm?"

David realized that she was looking for a serious answer, but he didn't think she could accept what he told her. He looked at Lena and said, "I would never have met your mother if I hadn't come home." He privately marveled that as a young man he had left the sirens singing in the West and come home to farm. He especially appreciated Margarette's conclusion:

Father is now seventy-seven years of age and until
this day he is working every day. We children
think a lot of our father, because he understands
and if there is anything we want to know or for help,

*he is the one we ask. If I ever gain as much knowledge
and intelligence as he has, I'll be satisfied. Father is
trying to give his children an education, because he
knows how handy it is in life.*

Margarette received an A for her efforts, and her parents agreed that she had done a fine job.

David and Lena were proud of Margarette who graduated from high school as an honor student. They sent her on to Madison Technical College for two years because Barneveld High School did not have the latest classes. She took a variety of studies including typing, commercial arithmetic, business, hygiene and child care, and cooking.

Both David and Lena missed her help and company on the farm, but the boys were old enough to be good help now, and Lena realized that their daughter would soon be finding a young man and settling down with her own family. As a matter of fact, Lena convinced David to buy a home for Margarette in Barneveld.

Margarette did find a young man named Julius Ray Osborn. The family all liked and admired her multi-talented beau. Ray, as they called him, was crazy for flying. He and a friend in Madison had even built an airplane together. During World War II he had served as a Navy electrician and then went to work at Badger Ordinance, north of Madison.

After he and Margarette were married, Ray continued his interest in flying. Unfortunately he died too soon, of a massive heart attack after taking off in his plane. He left his wife with four children at home to support. Typical of Margarette, she went to work, never asking for help. No one ever heard her complain.

Chapter 20

WALTER

Walter on the right, with his younger brother, Harold.

Margarette's younger brother was born in 1920. His birth was easy for Lena, and she and David marveled at their little boy who they called Walter after his grandfather. "A boy, what a wonder," David said, looking at his wife and child. The baby's name was a promise that Ol' Watt's stone barn and farm would stay in the family. The future of the farm was safe.

David was so bound up with his own feelings of pride that he neglected to question Lena when she wanted to see the doctor only a few months after Walter's birth. He figured that it was probably some complication that she was having. As they rode into town the next day, David realized that it was the baby that worried her. "He's fussy," she said. "He refuses to eat the way he should."

David had really tried not to believe that Walter was puny and sickly from the start, keeping them both awake and worrying Lena. At the doctor's office David looked curiously and rather impatiently around him at the folks with sniffles, coughs, and arthritis.

Lena seemed to be taking a lot of the doctor's time. Finally, the nurse came out. "Mr. Thomas, you may join your wife now."

The doctor had a certain look that David disliked, and Lena would not meet his eyes. The baby had a hole in his heart. "You can hear it," the doctor said. Wondering, David attached the stethoscope to his ears and leaned forward as the doctor placed the other end on Walter's little chest. The baby's heart was beating steadily, but with a slushy sound after each beat.

"What does this mean?" David asked.

Sounding very professional and detached, the doctor replied, "There is nothing we can do to repair the hole. It will affect his breathing all his life. You'll find him breathless if he exerts himself too much. If he lives, and there is no way we can predict how long he will live, he will learn to moderate his activities."

Lena bundled up Walter and walked out of the office. David followed at a slower pace. Not a word did they speak on the long, awful ride home. They both were struck dumb with despair and disappointment. That evening, after she had fed Walter, Lena came to David who held her close, still not knowing what to say.

The next day they went back to their routine. Both looked at their healthy four-year-old girl with different eyes. They also watched Walter, almost afraid to hold him and play with him as one would do with a normal child.

Walter had been a fussy baby, but he began talking and toddling almost as soon as most children did. If he became excited or began running around though, he soon started breathing with difficulty, and someone would suggest that he stop, or rest, or take it easy.

David brought him down to the barn when he was older where he learned to feed the calves and put down hay for the cows. He was an eager fellow and always started out doing a good job. After a while though, he seemed to slow down and then stop completely, literally, to catch his breath as an old man would do after too much exertion.

As David and Lena grew to love and understand their little boy, Walter learned to accept his place on the farm. He used his limited energies where he could. There was no place on their farm, or on any other farm for a lazy, do-nothing.

David and Lena knew that they treated Walter differently than their other children. David never whipped Walter, no matter how much he deserved it. Lena always had something for Walter to do around the house, so David grew to depend on Margarette for the help he needed in the barn. Lena's sisters said that they spoiled Walter in that way. Perhaps they did. It was hard to do any differently. Bright child that he was, Walter knew his father was a strict man, but he learned that his father would never strike him as he did Margarette and Harold.

■ ■ ■

As a child Walter played with his blocks, adding household items that seemed appropriate, spools from thread and odd nails and screws that he picked up. When he started school, Walter thrived on learning. What he lacked in energy seemed to be made up for by a desire to learn. He devoured the "how to" sections of magazines and newspapers. In his spare time he made things.

David feared this was all going to come to an end when Walter awoke one morning complaining of a sore throat. He insisted that he had to go to high school, so his parents gave in, allowing him and his younger brother, Harold, to take the car. That afternoon when they returned home, Walter went straight to his room. They found him asleep on the bed before dinner. His face was flushed, and he complained of his joints hurting. Lena began feeding him cool tea sweetened with honey. Then she boiled up a chicken and strained off the broth for him. By morning his fever was still raging, and they called the doctor.

Meanwhile, Lena bathed him with cool cloths, hoping to bring down the fever. His chest was covered with a rash like nothing they had seen before. "I'm afraid it's rheumatic fever," the doctor announced.

"Will he live?" Lena asked.

"I can't give you much hope," he said. Then seeing her despair, he added kindly, "You are doing everything you can to pull him through."

The doctor's words were a challenge to Lena. She did not go to bed for the next three days. "Just bring me water," she said. "I'll take his temperature down."

Harold was happy to miss school for a day to haul water and chicken broth to help his mother with Walter. Finally, the fever broke. Both Walter and Lena fell into a sleep that lasted a full day. David believed that he would get his boy back.

Although Walter was weak for a long time, all he wanted was to go to school. During his convalescence, David would visit with him every day, telling him about the farm. That was when Walter told him that he hoped to become an inventor.

"Inventors are mostly dreamers," David said dismissing the boy's aspirations.

"Cyrus McCormick had a very profitable dream. Thomas Edison and the Wright brothers also came up with useful inventions," Walter said. With that, he pulled out a fat little black notebook. Walter almost looked feverish again so David listened without protest.

"Look at this." Walter flipped through a few pages filled with carefully drawn figures. They looked like devices used on the farm for grinding coffee, shelling corn, and milking cows. Impatiently he paged through more drawings of what appeared to be light bulbs. "There," he said, "I'm designing a better cigarette, one that really tastes good. Charcoal is what we are using." He pointed dramatically. "We put some charcoal in front for the smoke to go through. Harold and I have been trying it out."

Walter stopped when he realized that he had gone too far by involving his younger brother. His father wondered just how much experimenting they had been doing.

"Why don't you concentrate on inventions that we can really use around the farm?" his father asked. Then he left the room, shaking his head and looking for Margarette.

■ ■ ■

It was a great day for all of them when Walter took off in the family car to attend a full day at Barneveld High School. Not content with a high school diploma, Walter continued his education with correspondence courses through the university.

David tried not to worry about Walter. There seemed enough to worry about on the farm. They had a terrible time keeping hired men. The good ones always wanted more money, and the bad ones skipped out as soon as the work got heavy and he really needed them. David did not talk about it much, but sometimes he was just desperate enough to go to the Madison unemployment office and hire drunks. Some of them were good workers after they dried out.

Once school was over for the year, Walter came down to the barn, looking for his father. It had been a long convalescence, and David feared that the boy might never be able to do farm work. Walter still moved deliberately, as if testing his endurance, but there was eagerness in his face that David appreciated. "I need a job," Walter blurted out breathlessly. "I know things. I'm good at working with the animals. I can help."

There he was, about David's height, but much thinner. At Walter's age, David was teaching school and dared to dream of going to the university and becoming a lawyer. David knew that the boy would not accept a careless answer. He thought for awhile, just looking him over and wondering. "I'm thinking about hogs," he finally answered.

"Hogs," Walter blinked.

"What do you think about raising a different breed of hogs? Think we could make some real money with them?"

Walter listened to what his father said and took it seriously, just as it was meant. He answered deliberately, "I think we can send away for some pamphlets from the university. That might be the best place to start. Then I will do some figuring on what we need and what we can make."

When David saw him pull the little black book out of his jacket pocket, he knew that Walter would work it out in time, and he did. The pamphlets laid out everything, from breed selection and farrowing to marketing. Walter and his brother built new pens with very little help from their father or the hired man. Then they made special farrowing crates guaranteed to keep the sows from killing their piglets. They sold off all the old hog stock and started anew.

For Walter, raising hogs was a kind of "invention" that provided monetary reward. Lena believed he was as proud of the first check for hogs as he was of his high school diploma. Some folks might say that he was stubborn about pigs, because he kept pigs long after the market had bottomed out. At only ten cents a pound, they lost a lot of money later on. But, both father and son felt that hogs were a part of the Thomas family tradition, and neither was about to change that.

Walter's skills with animals weren't limited to hogs, though. He watched the cows, driving them into the barn when their calving time was near, making sure the calves was born with no complications. He really understood animals.

Walter never married, but enjoyed the family life around him. Like his father, he delighted in an amicable audience. During dinner he talked about news events and asked the family their opinions, listening carefully to his nieces and nephews' views as well as the adults'. Walter described the new inventions he read about, amazing things like rockets that might just go to the moon, and high speed airplanes. He was especially fascinated by television's ability to send pictures through the airwaves.

The pigs were Walter's primary interest, and many years later his niece Diana became her Uncle Walter's special helper. They would go, hand in hand, down to the shed in the cold of winter and work with a farrowing sow. "Up and down, up and down," Diana related, fascinated with the miraculous challenges of birth. "She delivered some piglets. Then she got up and lay down again." Wildly gesturing, she explained, "We had to move fast to get the babies out from under her." When she was older, Walter showed Diana how to reach up inside a pig that was having difficulties and pull the little piglets out one by one.

When it came time for the children to do their homework, Walter was the one who sat with them and answered their questions, insisting that they do quality work.

It was his inventions, though, that set him apart from the rest of the family as an adult. He never stopped drawing and thinking about how to make things better. His nieces and nephews watched him putter from a distance. Then, when he was ready for a trial run, he seemed to want an audience. "Come on, Dad, he would call, "bring the kids."

I'm going to show you an airplane that will never crash," he announced one day. David gathered with the children in the side yard where he found Walter connected a round saucer-like thing with a vacuum cleaner motor.

Well, the "airplane" did not crash, mainly because it never got off the ground sufficiently to come down, but there were other ideas, like the hot air engine that could be run on water. When David looked at his son's drawings and studied his ideas, he wished that Walter had been able to go on to the University. He could have been an engineer. David understood what it was to have unrealized dreams.

Chapter 21

HAROLD

Harold with the rooster called Penny.

About a year after Walter's birth, Lena said to David, "I'll be having another child."

David could see the fear in her eyes as she broached this sensitive subject. She was thirty-nine and he was sixty. "When will it be born?" he asked as calmly as he could.

"Late summer," she said quietly. "I believe it will be another boy." He reached for her hand, and they shared a moment of hope and happiness.

David insisted that she see the doctor immediately. Little Walter was still doing poorly, and both feared for another sickly child. The summer was hot and dragged interminably. David did not feel that it was his place to act too concerned, or to inquire. Lena kept up with her chores without complaining, although she moved more slowly as the summer's heat became oppressive.

Early one morning in August, Lena woke her husband, "David, David," she said, "the baby is coming." But it was too early. Something was very, very wrong.

"Margarette," shouted her father, "Take care of your brother." Then he pounded on the hired man's door. "Lena's having the baby," he roared, "get the car warmed up and help me take her to the hospital." They drove quickly to town for the doctor, who agreed to meet them at St. Joseph's Hospital in Dodgeville. Lena's cries spurred the hired man over the road, faster than he had ever driven, oblivious to what little traffic there was. To David the ride was interminable—a ride through the dark tunnels of Hell with Lena's cries drowning out all sense and meaning.

At the hospital, David almost collapsed with relief. The nuns worked quietly and confidently to help Lena out of the car. Doc Morrison pulled in just behind them.

A nun directed David to a comfortable room. "Get some sleep," she suggested. "It will be sometime before your baby is born."

David must have dozed off for quite a time. When he awakened, the same nun brought a steaming cup of coffee and sat down with him while he drank it.

"Your wife is doing well," she said, "and your son will live." He took a deep breath as she went on, "He's so very small, coming early, you know. He and his mother will be staying with us for awhile."

Lena did not have to stay more than a week, but the baby needed time in the incubator to gain weight. Weighing only a little over two pounds at birth, he had a lot of growing to do. The hired man drove them to Dodgeville every day to hold the baby and admire his perfect little body. Lena's sister Ida brought Walter home with her during this difficult time.

She fed him so well that when he finally returned, he was quite a chubby little fellow.

After the baby came home, Lena and David went frequently to the doctor for checkups, not because they thought anything was wrong, but because they needed the doctor to confirm their feelings that they had a healthy baby. He assured them there was no problem. Lena was so relieved that she recovered quickly and was ready to help by harvest time. The baby thrived on his mother's milk and soon was helping her guide the cereal spoon to his mouth.

David was secretly very pleased that Lena had named the boy David, but he insisted that they call him by his middle name, Harold. As Baby Harold began to grow, David could not help but remember little Tommy, Lena's endearing first child. Tommy had always wanted to be with him in the barn, riding the wagons, and "helping" do chores. David had called him his "little shadow." David believed that he saw the same interest in this baby's eyes.

David took Harold to the barn as soon as the child could toddle down the hill. Sometimes Lena tracked them down and swooped the child up for some reason or other. Perhaps she wanted to be sure that nothing happened to Little David, as she often called him.

■ ■ ■

By the time Harold was going on five, Lena no longer worried about his health, and she knew the barn and farm chores drew him like a magnet. Besides, Margarette was usually helping to do the chores these days, and she kept an eye on the little tyke.

One day David was down by the barn assisting the hired man. He had broken an axle on the wagon and needed help unharnessing the horses, who were excited from the accident. David and the hired man turned to support the wheel before collecting the reins, when the horses bolted, dragging the harness and the wagon with them. The great big old white horse headed for the open gate just as Harold appeared to find out what all the excitement was about. Margarette, coming down to help, saw it all from above. She saw the horse charging forward. "Harold," she called, "Harold stop! Oh, stop. Come to me."

Harold, turned to look at her. Then, the horse stepped right on his back, pushing his little body down into the ground.

David heard Margarette scream, though he never heard a sound at all from Harold. Margarette reached the little boy first and scooped him up, running for the house.

David hurried up the hill as fast as he could. Walter kept repeating, "Harold's hurt, Harold's hurt." The house echoed with Lena's sobs, and David feared the worst.

They stretched out Harold's inert body on the bed. Lena and Margarette held a mirror up to his lips. He was still breathing. David felt his son's chest moving ever so slightly. He sat down on the bed, overwhelmed with emotion. "What about the doctor?" he asked.

Lena shook her head, "No, wait for now, he's breathing so steady." Mother and sister stayed with him all that afternoon until Harold finally opened his eyes, and Lena gently moved all his limbs. Then she asked David to get some of the liniment they used when the horses went lame. David watched as Lena carefully turned Harold over and rubbed on the salve. Harold did recover, and never had to go to the doctor.

■ ■ ■

It seemed to his parents that Harold was always getting in trouble. More often than not, it had to do with Walter. "Alright little brother, I have a job for you," he said. "It's part of my experiment. Just break open this little glass tube so we can get out the silvery stuff."

"But it's the thermometer!" Harold protested.

"Fraidy-cat, just do as I say and I'll show you something magical. I'll put it back together."

The mercury was fascinating, and delighted both boys until Walter collected it for further experiments and left Harold with the broken pieces of glass. His father was angry when he found the little boy playing with the broken thermometer.

"What did you do with the thermometer?" Harold's father thundered. Then, he chased him up the woodpile and spanked him soundly.

Eventually, Lena and David realized that Walter was often the instigator. Lena tried to be fair to Harold, and she encouraged Walter to stop getting his little brother in trouble. Luckily for Harold, David and Lena felt less inclined to punish Harold as they both got older and he got bigger and stronger.

■ ■ ■

Harold was still small when he and his big brother and sister helped their father build a reservoir around Lithium Spring. The children hauled a big pile of rocks and called it play for an hour or so. While they worked, David told them the story of how the spring got its name. His present plan was to run a pipe from the spring to the cow tank in the barn. They cemented the cow tank later on to hold the water better. Harold's appointed job every spring when he was still little was to get down and clean the slushy pipe hole.

One year the gypsies came up the road in their rickety cavalcade of beater cars, trucks converted to little houses, and horse-drawn wagons. There was even a tiny little trailer with colorful figures painted all over it. As foreign as they appeared, they might as well have been Egyptians.

David learned they were coming his direction from the hired man who met them on the road. The Thomases kept close watch, hoping the gypsies would pass them by, but the caravan turned into their pasture where there was a windmill to bring water for the cattle. David told the children, "If we let them alone, they will not bother us." Then he turned to Harold who had been watching the gypsies set up camp. "I need you to go down there and turn on the windmill."

Harold listened to his father and nodded his head, but he was remembering another story that Margarette told when she wanted to scare her little brother.

"Gypsies steal children, especially babies and little boys," she said, glancing at him. Then she told the story. "One day Mother and Baby Walter and I were coming home from Amacher Hollow, when we came upon a bunch of gypsies, all decked out in their fancy clothes. Mother said that the clothes were made out of table cloths and curtains they stole right off the clothes line. Some were riding horses and others pulled little wagon houses."

"Then Mother said to put the baby in the back of the wagon and cover him with a blanket. If they search, maybe they won't find him."

"My heart was pounding," Margarette said, "I was that scared. I hoped they wouldn't hear it. Mother and I held our breath as the gypsies went past, just looking straight ahead. We were lucky that time," Margarette said, looking significantly at Harold.

Actually, most folks believed that gypsies were more dangerous than the Indians. Generally folks had little contact with the gypsies, except at the county fair where they specialized in fortune-telling, fiddle-playing, and acrobatics. Harold knew that the gypsies ran all the concessions, and children were advised to steer clear of them.

Harold was unhappy when told he had to go down where the gypsies were camped. "Get going," his father said. "Just don't pay any attention to those gypsies." As he expected, the boy watched the strange company for a bit and then made a mad dash for the windmill. He ran back just as fast.

At supper time, he played the part of a conquering hero. "They look just like Indians except they wear fancy clothes." Harold explained. "One man with a sash around his waist winked at me as he watered his horses. I just nodded, real polite, and left, fast."

■ ■ ■

As soon as Harold could handle a team of horses, his father sent him down with the milk to what was now called the Jennieton cheese factory. Harold really enjoyed the job the first week, but this kind of farm work was to be done "everrrrry morning." The milk cans were heavy, and milk could not sit around and wait for good weather. Seven days a week, rain, snow, or shine, the trip had to be made.

His father believed that Harold was just a natural-born farmer, though when David set out to teach him, explaining everything, Harold barely listened.

"Let's us just do it, Dad," he said. He always wanted to be shown something, never told, just the opposite of Walter. David admitted the boy was a fast learner once he saw how something was done.

One summer David was proud to bring home a brand new corn shredder. He borrowed a little more than he had planned, but at least they would not need to pay someone else to make fodder for the cattle, and they could shell their own corn. He proudly called Walter and Harold, "Boys, this is a machine that I bought for you to operate. Let me explain how it works."

"I'll be ten soon, Dad, I can do it," Harold said, but there was a lot to learn before they were ready for the shredder. The boy rode with his father to cut and bundle the corn, then they walked the fields together putting the bundles upright.

By this time David had learned how best to teach Harold. They worked together that summer to cut the twine and bind the bundles so they would dry. In September they picked up the dried shocks in a wagon and headed home to feed them into the shredder.

The boys looked at each other with pleasure when their father announced, "Next year Walter will run the shredder and Harold can do the bundling."

■ ■ ■

Every year the children drove a herd of cattle up to the stockyards in Barneveld. "Just let them follow the leader. There's always one that wants to get there first," their father advised. The children were on foot, and their father rode in the milk wagon or the lumber wagon. It was about a mile and a half to the stockyard. Nobody had a truck to haul cattle in those days.

They usually sold a boxcar load of cattle every year. Steers, children and father headed north where Highway 18/151 is right now, past a junk pile, what is presently a golf course, then past Arneson's garden.

One year an ornery old cow got away from them and wrecked the garden. "Dang it, boys, get that cow out. I'll be hearing from Naomi Arneson for years about this," their father complained.

The children worked together to corner the cow, and with no further mishap, they arrived at the stockyard to pen up their animals. It was a relief to close the gate. They waited around the railroad station to see the stock safely loaded into the railroad car and on their way to the Chicago stockyards.

When it was time to sell hogs, they would set out together much the same way, to the railroad station and slaughter.

After the train left the station, David and the children went into town for ice cream cones. Annie Jorden who ran the restaurant would always give them an extra dip. There were also groceries to pick up for Mother. Before going home they stopped at the J.W. Prior Drug Store for Walter's medicine. It made for a good long day.

■ ■ ■

As Harold grew older and more confident, he liked to have fun and was always playing jokes. "He's just 'feelin his oats.'" his mother said.

"He's almost a man now," his father complained, "I don't think it's funny."

Nevertheless, Harold was irrepressible. He would walk up very quietly behind a friend and hit his knee into the back of theirs. Of course, the unlucky person would fall forward, and Harold would have a good laugh. He seemed to pick on the right people for that trick because they usually laughed too, and he never got into serious trouble.

Another little trick he perfected was again sneaking up behind a fellow and this time tickling his neck with a piece of grass. The victim would slap as if at a fly or other annoying bug. Finally, when the 'bug' wouldn't go away, he turned to find Harold grinning at him.

Years later as an adult Harold had great fun with his nephew Tom who was learning to drive the tractor. "I'll ride with you on the back wheel hub and help you out," Harold said.

The ride went well at first, and then the tractor started veering right and then right again. "What are you doing with this tractor, Tom?" Harold yelled.

Tom could not control it, so he cut the engine, and turned to face Harold, who was laughing like a maniac. "You, he shouted, you're doing something. I just know it."

Tom was right. Harold could reach the brakes from where he was sitting and was causing the tractor to "go crazy." Of course, they weren't going very fast and nobody got hurt.

Music was fun and as important to Harold as breathing. He loved making music so much that his father never denied him, especially since the boy seemed to realize that farm responsibilities came first. Then the war intervened and took precedence over both the farm and the music.

■ ■ ■

In 1942, it was impossible to ignore the war news, but World War II became very personal for them when Harold volunteered. His dream, like that of most young men of his age, was to be a fighter pilot, marking "strikes" on the side of the plane as he made the world safe from the Japs.

Sometime in the two weeks before his physical he copied the following poem, thinking he would set it to music. He gave it to his father just before he climbed into the bus headed to Milwaukee where he would receive his physical.

UNFURL THE STARS AND STRIPES
Though the skies be overcast,
Onward our ship will sail;
With 'OLD GLORY' o'er its mast,
Our country will prevail.

Let the thunder shock its stand
Or lightning tear its gown,
God will grasp it in His hand
And never let it down!

Unfurl the Stars and Stripes
Neath the heavens of the night,
And hold its proud ensign
In the midst of peaceful light.

Unfurl the Stars and Stripes
Its glory and its power,
Bless it with goodwill of man
And Freedom rich with valor.

Harold was in Milwaukee most of the day. He returned after supper, ravenously hungry and wild as a stallion in new clover. He gave his father a bear hug, "Dad, they said you were too old and needed my help on the farm." He slapped Walter on the back saying, "Walt, we're just going to have to build an airplane and fly on our own." And then he hugged his mother and Margarette together, yelling at the top of his lungs, "They won't take me! I have to stay home and work on the farm."

It was hard to tell if Harold was mad or sad. The family was happy to have him home, but David knew the boy regretted not being able to get a chance to fly. The next year Harold went up in an old biplane and thought about buying it for $1000. David almost wished he had. Later on Harold seemed content to go flying a couple of times with his brother-in-law, Ray.

Harold had no thoughts of going on to school. Margarette was the one who brought it up after he found he was ineligible for the army. "I am the worker," he said, to end the discussion before it began.

■ ■ ■

Harold did not just work on the farm, however. He continued to play music. David admitted that he had fostered the music. Long ago, Margarette ordered a ukulele and sheet music from the Arthur Godfrey radio show. Then there was a button accordion that ended up in the attic when Harold finally received the Gene Autry guitar he admired.

Even the traveling salesmen seemed to know they had a musician in their family. David bought a "tremolo" from one such man. You might call it a dulcimer today. David liked the way it sounded. Oh, those salesmen could make an instrument sound so fine. Harold never much played it, however, and he never had any use for the mouth organ either, though he could play that, too.

The Evanses gave Harold a fiddle, and every Saturday he drove to Middleton where he took violin lessons from Herman Falkenstein, a local celebrity who played fiddle on the radio.

When he grew older, Harold loved playing music with the fellows at nearby house parties, at Doyle's in Cobb, and in Madison. They even traveled as far as the Mississippi River doing gigs and getting home in time to watch the sun come up and do the milking. One band they had was called Smelcher's Hot Shots. It included Harold, Leo Loy, John Smelcher and Buddy Fletcher. By then, Harold had acquired a steel guitar.

He was rather cocky as a young man and liked to enter musical contests. Both David and Lena were proud of him. In one contest, Harold placed second out of over one thousand entries. In an "old fiddler's contest" in Madison, he came home with first prize.

When Harold married Amy Nelson and their children came along, Harold gave up a lot of his traveling and playing with the bands. That did not stop the music though, because Harold was always working on a new song. He never neglected the farm work. He just used his free time for music.

Sometimes of an evening he and Amy would gather up the children and head for Mineral Point to visit with Amy's brother, Abe, and his wife, Winona. Or they would drive to Barneveld where they visited with Margarette and her family. Amy carried whatever Harold was playing at the time, fiddle, banjo or guitar, and Harold carried the electric bass that he eventually taught Amy to play. On these happy occasions, the children fell over each other with excitement because they knew that they would be able to play with their cousins while their parents made music.

Occasionally, when David smoked his pipe after dinner, he reflected on his three children. He looked out at the stone barn so anchored to the bedrock of their farm. What would happen to it all? Amazingly, he concluded, it just might be his fun-loving, musical son who would carry on the Thomas stories and traditions.

Chapter 22

DAVID'S FINAL YEARS

David Thomas.

When David was alive, his family never thought to question him. A university-trained lawyer, he was their authority, the only one they needed. While he never actually practiced law in Wisconsin, many neighbors stopped in for legal advice because the suggestions he gave them were always sound and because he never charged them.

After David was gone, his children would remember certain things and wonder. Why did he give up practicing law? Why did he leave the West? Why did he burn his papers and books? Why was he was so set in his ways about card playing and dancing, never touching a card and never dancing a dance?

David mentioned once that out west he had seen cards and gambling bring tragedy. As for dancing, his children did see him jig a bit when the music was particularly lively at the Amacher picnics, but he never danced with his wife. He must have approved of music though, or he would not have purchased those instruments for Harold.

Another mystery about David was his life in the West. As a boy, Harold frequently found himself dreaming about leaving the farm. He wondered if he had gone west like his father, would he have ever returned to Wisconsin?

Margarette and Harold vividly remember an experience that might have insured that their father's past would remain a secret. David had decided to clean out the attic to use it for drying some produce. "Fire prevention," he said. As usual, Margarette and Harold followed his orders. They burned every book and letter that he fired out the attic window. At the time, they admired the stamps before they consigned the envelopes to the flames. Now, they wonder about the content of the letters.

Harold remembered one conversation that he had with his father down in the stone barn. Harold asked David about lawyering. "Do you ever miss being a lawyer, Dad?" he asked.

David did not respond right away. He just continued pitching hay down for the cows. Then he looked at Harold hard and said directly, "If I had it to do over again, I would not have given up being a lawyer."

Harold waited for him to continue, knowing there was more.

His father looked around slowly, taking in the solid walls and high rafters of the stone barn's hay loft, "I didn't want Father's stone barn to go out of the family." They never talked of it again, but David had made himself clear about Harold and the stone barn's future.

■ ■ ■

About this time Aunt Sadie came to visit from Pueblo, Colorado, where she had been running a boarding house. It was the same boarding house David had stayed in during the short time he was a lawyer in Pueblo. At first, the family enjoyed her company. She told wild tales of experiences with her boarders. David especially enjoyed spending hours talking about their youth on the farm.

Unfortunately, it was not long before the family realized that Aunt Sadie was living in a different world than theirs. She became obsessed with sweeping the kitchen, the walks, everywhere, even when there was no dirt to sweep. It was when she went to the shed and for no apparent reason brought back the ax, that David decided it was time for her to go back home to Colorado.

■ ■ ■

Much later in another attic cleaning effort, Harold found a notebook page crumpled up in a dusty corner. He saved it because the words on the page were about a barn and were written in his father's hand. It read:

How many a poor immortal soul have I met
well-nigh crushed and smothered under its
load, creeping down the road of life, pushing
before it a barn seventy-five feet by forty,
its Augean stables never cleaned, and one hundred
acres of land, tillage, mowing, pasture, and wood-lot…!
The better part of the man is soon plowed into the soil for compost….
The mass of men lead lives of quiet desperation.

The name *Henry David Thoreau* was scribbled below the lines. Harold read the passage over again that evening and put it away in his desk. He did not know anything about Augean stables, but he did know what an endless job it was to clean their own stables and dairy barn. Further, he somehow felt the words "quiet desperation" had special meaning for his father.

That same cleaning yielded another letter dated May 10th, 1953, a year before David's death. This letter gave Harold the feeling that his father was not Thoreau's typical man, "leading a life of quiet desperation," but rather a man who never compromised his values, living what he believed. The letter indicated that David had established a scholarship fund at his alma mater, the University of Wisconsin:

Dear Mr. Thomas:

*I have recently been informed of the
granting to me of $100 from the David D. Thomas
Scholarship Fund of the Law School of the
University of Wisconsin. Allow me to extend
my sincere thanks to you. I shall do my best
to justify the confidence reposed in me.*

*Sincerely,
Pertti J. C. Lindfors
3rd-Year Law Student*

■ ■ ■

Life on the Thomas farm was rather uneventful in the late forties and early fifties. That was probably why the family was so excited about an upcoming pageant. Sunday, August 10, 1952, had a big circle around it on their calendar. Mrs. Steiner Swenson of the Blue Mounds Advancement Association was rumored to have outdone herself on a pageant planned for that day.

No one in the family was personally acquainted with Mrs. Swenson, but the pageant/drama, which promised to unfold the history of Blue Mounds, sounded interesting to everyone. Harold looked forward to hearing the Knutson brothers, who would be providing between-the-scenes music. "Have the picnic lunch ready after chores so that we can get to the Mound in time to visit and watch the games," he told Amy. Walter decided to clean and wax the car.

Amy had heard some of her neighbors were searching their attics and closets in hopes of finding authentic wear for the pioneers, miners, Indians, and soldiers in the pageant. She was ready for an outing as well, and began planning the lunch with Lena. Diana, Harold and Amy's first daughter, was tickled at the prospect of seeing other children her age and kept asking, "How many days until the picnic?" She told her dolls again and again all about the plans for a picnic on Blue Mounds.

The day for the pageant was a perfect one. By the time the brilliant sun was high in a cloudless blue sky, the chores were finished. The family cleaned up as if for church, then loaded up the car and piled in. Walter drove, with Amy and Harold squeezed in beside him. In the back, David and Lena held Diana.

The traffic was considerable. They learned from the *Capital Times* later that, "An estimated 1,300 persons thronged the park, including the home folks of this area, former residents, out-of-town visitors and descendants of pioneers of Pokerville and Blue Mounds." They were lucky to have started out early so Walter could get through the traffic and find a good place to picnic and watch the performance. They spread their blankets near Margarette and Ray.

Mrs. John Minx, owner of the park concession atop the Mounds, was busy selling lemonade. Mrs. Steiner Swenson narrated the two-hour pageant/drama. The two of them had done most of the research for the presentation, and were relieved that the weather was perfect.

The Thomas family reveled in a day together away from farm responsibility. Amy and Lena's deviled eggs and sandwiches tasted much better on the Mound than they did at home. Friends and relatives stopped by, providing welcome interruptions. David and Lena enjoyed the passing scene in lawn chairs.

"The Winnebagos named this place *Weekaukja*," explained Diana's grandfather.

"Weeja," the little girl repeated.

"*Weekaukja*," her grandfather corrected. "It means a high place with a wonderful view."

"*Weehaukja, Weekaukja*, Weeja, I'm an Indian girl!" Diana danced around the blanket.

"Hush now. Come sit on my lap. Look up at the stage. They are about to begin the pageant," her mother said.

Mrs. Swenson began her narration. "Our hope is that with the following pageant we will successfully link the yesterdays with today." David's eyes never left the stage as legendary figures came to life in front of him—the first settler, Ebenezar Brigham, and the first family, the Eben Pecks.

Diana was enchanted by the Indians in full regalia who rushed onto the stage with the intention of putting a stop to the mining in the area. She drew close to her father and watched as the white men "built" Fort Blue Mounds for protection. The next scene held everyone's attention as Mrs. Swenson told the story of the Hall girls.

"Down in Illinois the marauding Indians terrorized folk and captured two young girls whom they held for ransom." She paused for effect, "The countryside was in an uproar of fear and indignation. Colonel Henry Dodge collected the ransom from some of his wealthy friends and came to the fort to exchange it for the two girls."

Diana crawled into Harold's lap and watched for the next development. One of the little Hall girls did not look much older than Diana. As the Indians pushed two girls forward, Colonel Dodge came to center stage with two thousand dollars, a great deal of money in those days. The audience applauded loudly in relief as he handed it to the Indian chief and reached for the girls. Diana looked up at her father, "I'm so glad they went back to their mama and daddy." Harold smiled and gave her a hug.

David had a good laugh when Mrs. Swenson introduced the next chapter in the history of Blue Mounds, "Pokerville, founded about 1840, earned its name from the miners who, unrepressed by the civilizing influences of the fairer sex, drank and gambled in unrelieved freedom when they weren't mining for lead."

"My first teaching job was in Pokerville," David reminded the family in a loud whisper, as they watched the "fort" being rearranged on stage to depict, not a school house, but a saloon. The actors drank quietly and played cards until "Slippery Dick" pushed open the swinging doors, and in true Western villain style, proceeded to start a fight with just about everyone on stage. The actors almost drowned out the narration with all their shouting.

Then out of nowhere there was a shot, and "Dick" fell to the floor, face down. At this point, the audience clapped and shouted so much in their delight that Mrs. Swenson just threw up her hands and directed the actors to change the set.

Harold watched his mother and Amy laugh with the rest of them, but the women really enjoyed the musical parts of folk dancing and fiddling the most. They sang the old songs along with the rest of the audience.

At the end of the pageant, Mrs. Swenson introduced descendants of the old settlers while the picnickers packed up their baskets. Some folks had come from as far away as Long Beach, California, and New York City. Everyone agreed it was a most enjoyable outing.

■ ■ ■

In 1954—two years after the pageant, David had a stroke. An ambulance took him to Madison General Hospital. Lena stayed with him day and night for two weeks. From the moment he was struck down and taken away, the house was strangely quiet. The rooms echoed without his authoritarian voice. His empty chair at the kitchen table mocked them, asking what they were going to do now.

Amy, David, and Walter went to Madison every other day to relieve Lena. They stayed as long as they could, but there was no change, and each day they saw less hope in Lena's eyes. They would go back to the empty house and change into barn clothes. The hired man had done what he could, but there were more chores to do.

Each day without David seemed to be harder. One morning as he started his chores, Harold turned around, expecting to see his father's stooped form heading down to the barn.

If such a thing were possible, the stone barn seemed emptier and more lonesome than the house. As David had become older, he had never stopped working. Sometimes, all bent over and carrying his water jug, he would go out to cut weeds. Too often, he was so slow and so deliberate that Walter and Harold became impatient and took over the job he had assigned himself. Now, both men cursed themselves for causing their father pain.

Harold remembered his father's kindness with little Diana. David would take short, slow walks perfectly suited to a little girl. One time they would head for the windmill down by the machine shed. Another time they would stop at the bench by the wood pile. Grandpa David would tell a story, and Diana would listen very attentively, just as Harold had listened to his father's stories over the years.

Diana reminded Harold later, after she had graduated from college and was teaching first grade, that her grandfather's stories about teaching school were the ones she remembered the best, especially the one about taking a gun to school.

Walter wrote in "A Son's Tribute to a Father" published in *The Wisconsin State Journal*, "For two weeks the family put up a valiant fight, never losing hope until the last day that he would regain consciousness, and that recovery would come."

Sadly, David never did regain consciousness. He passed away on Saturday, February 20, 1954. He was ninety-four years old. In his family's eyes there had never been a finer man, a better father, and a more caring husband.

■ ■ ■

After the funeral Harold was confused and unhappy in a way that he failed to understand and did not want to discuss. Amy would have to call him to get up in the morning. Once up, he did chores mechanically. It was the most difficult time in his life. Lena was grieving as well. Walter hardly spoke. They sat at the table with their breakfast coffee and waited for something that never happened, and never would. Amy would finally break this reverie, and the men would head for the barn. Lena would clear the table and begin the dishes.

■ ■ ■

Gradually the family took up the life that lay ahead of them. Walter and Harold worked on the farm, little Doug was born, the children grew like weeds, and the farm just kept asking more of them, as if it had a life of its own. Eventually, Amy and Harold went back to playing music. They made up a band of their own called Country Drifters. Amy sang and played the bass and Harold played any instrument the music seemed to require. He took up yodeling as well, which the audience always enjoyed.

Harold learned to yodel from his mother. One day when he was a boy, Harold had finished his chores and was playing around with his new guitar in the empty stone barn. He had tuned up and was getting into a very personal rendition of "Edelweiss," when his mother peeked in the barn door. She almost danced over the floor in her delight with the music. "That music wants yodeling," she said. "Let me show you how to do it," Harold nodded his head and continued playing until she held out her hand, telling him to stop.

Lena began to yodel as she had done in Switzerland. Harold had never heard her yodel except at the Amacher picnics. Now she was enjoying performing just for him. She wanted him to learn, and she was a very good teacher, delighting in her son's talent.

Amy and Harold made some money with their music. They played at bars, clubs, homes, and nursing homes, wherever the audience enjoyed Country Western with a Swiss accent. Amy did a fine job with the vocal solos and the beat on the bass, and Harold wrote songs. Of course, they never took the children. Folks were drinking, and youngsters belonged at home.

After David died, Lena, Walter, and Harold formed a legal partnership to manage the farm. They felt that their father's hopes and dreams for the farm and the stone barn would be safe with them. It was Walter's idea to do this. After David's death, Walter's feelings about the farm were especially strong, and protecting the stone barn became almost an obsession.

FAMILY LIFE ON
THE FARM 1946-1965

Harold on the 1937 Model A, John Deere. Photo by author.

Amy and Harold had married in 1946. Because David and Lena believed that a young married couple needed privacy, they fixed up a separate apartment for the newlyweds on the second floor. It seemed like a sensible arrangement until little Douglas caught the measles in third grade and Lena had an operation for a "rupture."

The need to care for one another during illness changed their living arrangements. After that, they all decided to eat together, and then they just logically lived together as the extended family they were.

Amy helped Margarette and Ray with their little girls before her own children came along. Amy was good with children, but she was not born a farmer. She had grown up in Mineral Point helping her mother who worked as a cook at the Royal Inn.

In fact, at the age of five, Amy did not even know what a cow looked like. She and her friend walked home from school past the telephone office one day. In the large yard surrounding the office, they saw some very big black and white animals. "Elephants," they declared to each other. What else could they be, but elephants without trunks?

"Maybe they're girl elephants," Amy's friend suggested wisely. Scared and confused, they headed home as fast as they could.

Amy's mother laughed when she heard their story. "Nothing but a few heifers," she said. "They're just little cows, not elephants at all."

However, in spite of her upbringing, Amy learned fast and worked with Harold and Walter when they needed her. She began a garden, learned to feed the chickens and to clean the hen house. She fed the hogs. She helped with haying, and always somewhat reluctantly, shoveled silage.

Harold never thought too much about it, but Amy was set aback by their lack of modern conveniences. Any hot water they needed was heated on the wood stove in the kitchen or in a "donut" heater. Harold expected her to cook on the wood burning stove and keep the oil burners filled in the bedrooms so the family would be cozy at night. During the winter when it was icy and she did chores outside, Amy scattered wood ashes for traction. Although Harold really did not want Amy to have to work as hard as his mother had, he and Walter needed Amy more and more as they expanded their beef herd.

Some big families have trouble getting along. The Thomases did not, and Harold credited it to Amy's good nature. She spoke her mind when needed, but she never argued or fussed over little things. Her best quality was that she was a jokester, just like Harold. They could always laugh together over just about anything, good or bad.

■ ■ ■

Amy and Harold's first child was almost a firecracker. Diana was born on the fifth of July, 1947. The drive to Dodgeville's Saint Joseph's Hospital on the Fourth of July would always be vivid in Harold's mind. It was just about dark, and as he drove Amy to Dodgeville, he could see the various little communities along the way setting off their fireworks.

By the time they arrived, Amy was very anxious. Harold had tried to reassure her, but he was not at all certain how fast little babies came. At the hospital the nurses sped his wife to a room while Harold paced the halls.

Soon after midnight the doctor strode up and shook his hand, "Congratulations, it's a beautiful little girl, and Amy is doing very well."

Their next child, Jeannie, came on May 26, 1949. Amy and Harold had looked forward to the birth of another child, and they were more relaxed, having gone through the experience. If they had consulted some of the books Amy planned to read, they would have realized that each birth is unique and wonderful in its own way. This time they went to Madison General Hospital.

Jeannie's given name was Regina. Amy had found her name on one of the radio "soaps" called "Back Stage Wife" that Grandma Lena enjoyed. The family liked the sound of the name, but Diana could not pronounce it, saying "Jena, Jena," to call her little sister, and so they called her "Jeannie" ever since.

Harold and Amy's boy was born in March 5, 1951. Harold celebrated Doug's birth with Margarette's husband, Ray, who also had a passel of girls. They celebrated again when Ray's son, Tom, was born four years later. The two boys became inseparable, as good as brothers.

Doug was all boy. He delighted and astonished them with his exploits. He was four when he poured gasoline on the house cat. He did not seem to have any malicious inclinations. He just did it, leaving his mother to wash the animal.

One day his mother found him putting clothes pins on the cat's tail. "Why?" she asked, after paddling him. "Why did you do these things to cats?"

"I just wanted to see if I could," Doug sobbed. When he was a little older, not content with these exploits, Doug experimented with cats by throwing them off the top of the corncrib.

"I'm doing an experiment," he said looking wisely at his Uncle Walter. "I want to see if cats really do always land on their feet. And, I want to see if they have nine lives."

His mother paddled him again, admonishing him to learn to get along with cats. "There will be no more torturing the poor things," she said sternly.

Doug did eventually make peace with cats. He learned what a powerful ally they could be against rats which he despised with a passion.

Harold and Amy's last child, Maggie, was born in Madison General Hospital in 1956. They named her Margaret after her great-grandma, Margaret Kendrick, and her Aunt Margarette. Maggie loved helping her mother plant potatoes and watching her father bring in the cows for milking, but unfortunately her schooling would interfere with these activities.

Maggie had a hard time with classes, especially at first. Amy finally allowed Maggie to take her favorite stuffed rabbit to school. The teacher had sense enough to allow the rabbit to stay as Maggie's companion until the strangeness of school wore off.

Harold took the children to school in the morning and they rode the bus home at night. One particular morning touched a cord in Harold's heart. "I don't want to go to school. Don't make me go to school," Maggie lamented.

"You're not sick," her father reminded her gently. "You really need to go to class now."

There were tears in his eyes as he watched her walk slowly through the big double doors of the schoolhouse.

Their last child might have been a bit spoiled, because at first her older sisters treated her like a doll. They almost wore her out playing "little mother" while changing her clothes and diapers. As she grew up, Maggie became a pest to her big brother, Doug, because she felt it was her duty to tell on him, especially when he pestered the cats.

The children enjoyed riding their bikes together, although going into town was strictly forbidden. One late Saturday morning Harold came in to look for some help in the barn. Amy was washing clothes. "I'm busy," she said. "Come to think of it, I haven't seen the children since breakfast."

"Well, it's not likely that we could lose four children just like that," Harold commented. Amy began calling for the children when Harold pushed past her and hailed Walter. He hadn't seen them either, not since early chores.

The men headed the car to town, trying not to think the worst. They had driven around for a half hour when Walter said, "Margarette and Ray's." And that was where they found the children, playing with their cousins. There was no room in the car for the kids and the bikes, so the children continued their lark by riding home. Punishment was forgotten as they put away their bikes and busied themselves with chores. Only Walter was disgruntled with Amy and Harold. "You two aren't strict enough," Walter said.

"You may be right there," Harold said, but he didn't always agree with Walter's ideas.

■ ■ ■

Amy was good at keeping the children in line. She enjoyed telling them stories about the farm and the woods. The story that always made the family smile was about the old John Deere tractor. The children had the story memorized, but they made their mother retell it many times.

The story was called, "The Putt-putt-a-putt that Wouldn't Putt," and it took place on a farm very much like theirs. The main characters were Putt-a-putt, the two-cylinder tractor, and Tippy, the dog. Every day the farmer called his dog and headed down to the barn to start up the tractor. The farmer opened the petcocks, letting out puffs of air, which caused the dog to bark.

"Putt-a-putt-a-putt," the tractor said, and Tippy barked like crazy. Then the farmer turned the big flywheel crank on the side of the two-cylinder engine.

Soon Tippy barked when the farmer just reached over to open the petcocks.

"Putt-a-putt-a-putt," the tractor said.

"See," the farmer joked, "we need Tippy to start the tractor," and he waved good-by to his children and his wife and Tippy. Then he roared out into the fields.

One day the farmer headed to the barn. Tippy was nowhere to be seen. The farmer called him once or twice and climbed into the tractor seat. He tried to start the engine, but Putt-a-putt wouldn't putt. The farmer went to find his hired man, who was a whiz at engines. The hired man took out a variety of tractor parts, cleaned them and put them back, but the farmer still could not start the tractor.

The farmer's wife came down to look at Putt-a-putt, and the farmer's children came down to watch. Still nothing happened. Finally, the farmer's little boy said, "We need Tippy to bark."

Everybody laughed, but the children went looking for Tippy. They called and they called and finally they could hear Tippy running toward them. "Tippy, Tippy!" they shouted, hugging and patting the excited dog. "Where have you been? Putt-a-putt won't start."

"Bark, Tippy, bark," they yelled, and Tippy barked.

All eyes turned to Putt-a-putt. The farmer grinned and tried once more to start the engine.

"Putt, putt, a-putt, a-putt," Putt-a-putt said. Everyone clapped except for the farmer, who was busy driving the tractor out to a field that needed to be cultivated. He laughed and called back to Tippy to stay close by.

Harold loved Amy's ability to bring their old tractor to life. She also entertained the children with spooky stories at night. While the children were young, Harold could see no need for television, although they all enjoyed the radio.

■ ■ ■

All the Thomases were partial to dogs. Tippy, of Putt-a-putt fame, was talented, but another dog, Trixie, was lots of fun too. She went everywhere with Harold. The kids took a great photo of her on the lawn mower. They claimed she could mow better than they could.

The Thomases also had a pig that thought she was a dog. One night rather late, Walter and the girls came into the kitchen loaded with squealing piglets. Diana announced importantly, "The sow would not let down her milk, and the little ones are starving."

Amy pulled out a wooden crate and put an old towel in the bottom. "I'll mix up some milk powder, and you can try to feed them."

After an exhausting night, only one piglet was alive. Jeannie called the piglet Sparky after the name on the milk powder container.

Sparky grew up behind the wood stove in their kitchen. When she grew too big, they moved her to the doghouse, and ultimately to the barnyard with the other pigs. When the children came home from school, Sparky would run to greet them at the gate, just like a dog. In the evenings when they paused before bedtime on the porch, there was Sparky with the family, relaxed and comfortably curled up at the bottom of the steps.

There was only one dog Harold did not like, a Gordon Setter. Doug favored him at first and called him Boots. No one realized until he bit Diana that the dog was determined to live up to his name. He was obsessed with guarding Doug's boots. When Diana went to get the boots in a misguided attempt to help her younger brother, the dog bit her lip so badly that she needed stitches.

Several days later Doug came home from school and went to put on his chore boots. He threw sticks to distract the dog, but he was not fast enough and Boots opened up his arm from wrist to elbow. The dog was gone the next day. Doug declined to tell the whole story. When asked about what happened to Boots, he would only repeat, "Enough is enough."

All the children had adventures with the animals. Even today, Diana, a first grade teacher, tells her school-children the story of a pig that took a ride down into the barnyard on Diana's back. It seems Uncle Walter was feeding the pigs outside the granary. He called to the big animals, which were asleep across the way.

As Diana flopped down on her sled and started down the hill from the house to the barn, a big fat sow walked across her path. Diana could neither stop nor turn out of the way, so she just sped ahead. The pig fell on to Diana's back, and they trundled down the hill together. Just as they reached the ramp to the haymow, the pig finally scrambled off the sled. Diana's school-children always enjoy the picture of their teacher sledding with a sow.

Perhaps their strangest pets were the goldfish that turned up in the cow tank. It was a mystery to them all where the fish came from. Amy believed that Harold put them there, and he believed it was the hired man. Eventually, only one goldfish survived. Jeannie checked on the remaining goldfish every day. She was fascinated by how fast it grew, eventually as big as a flounder. "Houge, houge," she would say. "Huge," they would correct. She would offer the fish bread crumbs, and it came to her fingers, the perfect pet.

The animals, most of them, gave the family a great deal of pleasure, but it was music that brought them together. They did not get a television until the sixties, so they played music in the evenings. At one time or another, Harold taught all the children to play the guitar.

Often he would start playing one of Amy's favorite songs on the steel guitar. She would come in to sing a little. Then Harold would look at Amy and wink. Picking up his fiddle he would slowly begin the first few bars of "The Cherry Blossom Special," a popular railroad tune. It was not long before all the children gathered, from Diana to little Maggie, who would keep time on a pan if they let her.

Sometimes Harold and Amy recorded their music. It was great fun to play it back and listen to some of their wild improvisations. Usually they played all the children's country favorites: Johnny Cash hits for Doug, June Carter for Diana, "Mockingbird Hill" for Jeannie. At the end of the evening Amy and Harold often harmonized with a favorite love song.

Chapter 24

PLAY AND HARD WORK

Stone barn with hay bales.
Photo by Jim Ballard.

Margarette and Ray Osborne's eight children were often at the farm. They hid behind the woodshed when it was time to go home, hoping they would be forgotten. Tom, in particular, almost lived there, coming after school and on the weekends. He baled hay, helped with the cattle and pigs, and repaired buildings with never a thought of pay.

The cousins enjoyed the stone barn as they would a giant playhouse. For Harold their shouts and laughter brought back the days when Margarette would perform for him and Walter, swinging, walking the beams, and cavorting like a circus lady.

The children climbed up and down the chutes used to drop hay bales from the upper mow to the cattle mangers below. Close to the peak of the barn the old hay fork rail still ran from one end to the other. When the hay was stacked high enough for a soft landing, they went hand-over-hand on the rail, and then jumped or fell screaming with laughter into the stacks of hay bales underneath. Sometimes, however, they would try the hand-over-hand trick without many hay bales underneath.

Mavis, Ray and Margarette's daughter, once missed a hand-over hand-hold on the rail and fell. There was little hay on the barn floor to soften a fall. Her Uncle Harold stepped in, by chance, and watched with the children in silent horror as Mavis fell.

He caught her and hugged the little acrobat to his chest as he let out the breath he had been holding. It was luck, just good luck, that he was there at the right time.

The kids could not resist climbing the elevator used to move the bales to the upper level of the barn. Once at the top, they straddled the smooth aluminum sides. Down they slid to the ground, squealing with pleasure. When Amy caught them, she questioned their safety, but it seemed a shame to spoil their fun.

Sometimes when working down below in the barn, Harold heard the children scurrying around upstairs. Or he heard jumping and realized the girls had found some hay twine and were skipping rope. Occasionally, one gave a shout, and they all gathered to look at a mother cat and her new kittens, safe and comfortable in their bed of hay. The boys liked to build tunnels and forts where they played hide-and-seek. This was especially fun when it was rainy outside and they could be safe and warm in the barn.

One day when it was particularly miserable outside, Harold went to the hayloft with the intention of having a little fun. The kids were imagining great adventures hiding from each other in the hay tunnels. From the shelter of the barn, Harold watched the lightning play across the sky, and then he turned to find the children. He looked carefully for some movement. It was quiet for a bit, and then he saw a bale tip slightly. He pounced on Jeannie, who first shrieked like a stuck pig and finally settled into a relieved hug. "Let's go in for dinner," Harold shouted to the other children, and led the way through the driving rain to the house.

It was not just the barn that attracted the children to the farm. Margarette's daughter Evelyn has bittersweet memories of the horses Walter put out to pasture because they were too old to work or ride. Evelyn adopted them as her own and rode the school bus out to the farm everyday after school to feed them some oats or apples. Often she combed their manes and talked to them.

One day she got down from the bus, loaded up a small bucket of oats and headed for the pasture. Even from a distance she could tell something was wrong. The horses knew her schedule, and they were not at the fence. She called. They did not come. She walked the pasture and found the fence secure. Someone had moved them.

The first person she saw back at the barnyard was the hired man. "Where'd you put the old horses?" she asked.

Without a thought he answered, "They were loaded this morning and shipped to the processing plant." He saw her disbelief and confusion and added, "You know, Walter sent them to the butcher place."

Realization overwhelmed Evelyn, "My horses," she sobbed. "Uncle Walter never told me." Crying with the horror of what she saw as betrayal, she headed for the house and the comfort of her Aunt Amy.

■ ■ ■

On Friday nights Harold became accustomed to going to Ray and Margarette's to watch the boxing matches on their television. He always brought the kids with him. They looked forward to it as their "fun night" for the week. The children played, and Ray and Harold tried to pick the winner of the boxing match.

Besides watching TV, the family enjoyed playing board games. Chinese checkers was a favorite they played on weekends until long after midnight. Margarette's sister-in-law and her family often came to make it a big family party. That was when Margarette made a couple batches of popcorn and fudge.

As Harold's family rode back to the farm, the children would become really quiet. Harold stopped the car and the family got out. "Now it's off to bed for you," he teased.

Usually it was Maggie who piped up, "Daddy, look at the millions and millions of stars."

Harold looked up then, and they would all try to help Maggie count the stars. "Can you find the Dippers tonight?" her sisters asked. Diana and Regina showed her the Dippers, and then they looked for Orion and Cassiopeia.

Harold never failed to be intrigued by the idea of galaxies far, far away, perhaps peopled with folks just like them. He was fascinated by the wonder and beauty of it all. "You can't see stars like this in town," he said as he and Amy pushed the children toward the house and bed.

The children never questioned their responsibilities on the farm. It was Doug, however, who came to realize he was really needed. He did take up some Future Farmers of America activities in high school, but he never even asked about joining football or basketball, or any activities that the town boys enjoyed. He knew he was needed on the farm. He loved working with cars and trucks, however.

There was a rusty old Studebaker behind the shed. Trees had grown up through it. It had not run for fifteen to twenty years. One afternoon Doug and Tom were helping Walter and Harold stack bags of feed for the pigs. They piled the heavy bags ever so nicely. Then Doug began, "Uncle Walter, you know that old car sittin' down in the weeds?"

"Yup," Walter answered, not really surprised to have the subject brought up. The boys had been studying that old car for the last few weeks. The grass was all beaten down around it.

"What's wrong with the thing?" Tom asked.

"The timing went out on it," Walter said. "Maybe something is wrong with the transmission." He paused, enjoying their enthusiasm, "Go ahead, tinker with the darn thing."

Harold smiled and nodded his head. The boys did not need more encouragement. They took out the transmission and found nothing wrong. Next they tackled the engine. They could not do any damage. They either fixed it or they didn't. Finally, they realized the timing gear did need replacing. A junk yard in Mineral Point had just the right part, but they still could not get the car started.

Then Doug had an idea and pulled the tractor down by the car. He connected the car to the tractor with a belt and adjusted the timing order on the sparkplugs. Then he "borrowed" a battery from the tractor. This time the car came to life. He immediately called up Tom, "Tom, I got it started. Come on over!"

"Oh yeah? I'll be right there." They lost no time in putting dual wheels on the car, setting a milking stool in where the seats had been torn out, and driving it all over the hay fields. The only mistake they made was to cut the roof off so they could drive around in open, convertible style, which limited them to driving on sunny days.

Harold readily accepted when the boys offered to take him for a ride. It was bumpy and exciting with the wind rushing through his hair.

The boys did get in trouble with Walter though. They drove on a "borrowed" battery, and more often than not it was from Walter's tractor. One time as they roared through the fields, they hit a bump, sailed to a rough landing, and rolled over what felt like a big rock. It was the battery, which had bounced out and landed in front of the car. Walter was not pleased. The boys had to pull a lot of weeds to pay for that mistake.

Tom and Doug were inseparable. Together they felt that they could do anything, even paint the ends of the stone barn. Harold had been lamenting the cost of the project.

"Oh, Uncle Harold," "Oh, Dad," they said simultaneously, "we'll do it for you."

"Well," he pondered, "it's rather high." However, nothing deterred them, and Harold bought the paint the next time he went to town.

It took the two boys over a week to paint the ends of the stone barn, and Amy fretted the entire time, especially when she learned that, finding their ladders too short, they had to paint the peak lying on the slippery slate tiles on the roof. Actually, Amy gave Harold the "Dickens" for putting them up to it. "Too dangerous," she said.

After the ends of the barn were painted and the boys were safely back on the ground, Harold questioned them about their safety precautions. "Well," said Doug, "Tom put some twine around me and held on while I did the painting." Amy and Harold both jumped in to point out how foolish it was to depend on twine to save someone from falling at that height. "I know," Doug answered calmly, "but it did make us feel safer."

■ ■ ■

When the children come home now, the one thing that they always talk about is filling up the stone barn with bales, year after year after year. After they filled the barn over halfway, they put the elevator up to the far opening, and Amy came from the house to help. She put the bales from the wagon on the elevator which carried them to the children and the hired men who were in the hay loft. These were big bales to handle, especially for little girls. This was before the small bales one gets from a throw-baler today. The children lugged and tugged the bales until they stacked them just right. Walter saw to precision stacking.

Walter always supervised putting hay in the barn. He made sure that it was bone-dry. It terrified him to think that spontaneous combustion caused by damp hay might consume their precious barn. Once, he even said it was criminal to use such a magnificent structure to store hay.

The children remember the fun they had on the farm, but they remember as well a serious, almost somber note that resonated from their encounters with Uncle Walter.

Their bachelor uncle had the final word on everything relating to the farm, and he was not chary about expressing himself, especially when it came to what he regarded as his most valued treasure, the stone barn. For example, Tom once drove the hay wagon into the hay mow, hitting the side of the doorway, not hard, just a little bump.

"Tarnation, can't you numbskulls ever learn to drive? You have just taken one hundred years off this barn," Walter growled.

Often when he was in a better mood and they were done baling hay for the day, Walter explained just why it was that he viewed the stone barn as a great work of art. Better than anyone in his family, he understood the fine engineering that enabled the barn to withstand more than a century of exposure and abuse.

"Take a real look at the arches. Do you know how many different kinds there are on our barn? Do you know how they *work*?" He waited for an answer.

"Tell us, Uncle Walter," someone would request, and he always did.

"These arches won't collapse because the stones are *cantilevered*, cantilevered," he repeated. "One end of the stone is fixed in compression with the vertical support and the free end is held in tension, ultimately by the keystone. These arches will last forever."

Then he added with great satisfaction, "It's not magic or happenstance, it's engineering."

Chapter 25

IT'S A DIFFICULT LIFE

Walter in front of their 1936 Plymouth.

Life on the farm revolved around cattle and making hay. The family used and repaired the equipment they had. Modern equipment came slowly if at all. Harold and Walter knew about fancy tractors with covers and fans, even air conditioning, but they never envisioned buying them.

One particular weary, hot day in July when perspiration and bits and pieces of hay conspired to make them miserable, Walter was driving the tractor and pulling the baler. Doug and Harold were stacking bales. They looked up to see a man calling and running across the field.

"Stop the tractor," Harold shouted to Walter. Walter slowly let the engine die down to a startling silence.

"What's the matter? he sputtered. "It's supposed to storm tonight. We need to get these bales into the barn."

There was something more pressing than hay bales this time.

The man, who on closer examination was Albert Miller, the town cop and a cousin of Margarette's, looked sharply at thirteen-year-old Doug and then turned to Harold. He did not say anything until he got up close. "Ray crashed his plane, Harold," he said. "I'm afraid that he's dead."

Walter climbed down from the tractor. "Where?" he asked Albert.

"Mineral Point," he said quietly. "He and that dog, Cricket, and his half-brother. They went up about five hundred feet, and then just came back down. Ray must have had one of those blackout spells of his. Margarette's at home."

"Doug!" Harold called. As the boy came up to the men, Harold said, "We need to take a ride to Mineral Point." Albert went back to his car, Walter started up the tractor again, and they rode the hay wagon back to the barnyard. Walter pulled the car out and Harold advised Amy to get ready to help Margarette. They believed the girls should stay home and not go to the airport. Walter drove, and Harold sat in the back seat with Doug.

Harold knew he needed to tell Doug what happened to his uncle before they arrived at the airport. As he struggled to find the right words to explain the tragedy, Ray's life flashed through Harold's head. Ray was a good friend and a fine man, as well as a wonderful husband and father. He was a successful electrician. He had just turned fifty.

There was a lot of sadness to share with Margarette and her adult children, Beverly, Evelyn, Mavis, Janet, and those at home, Shirley, Phyllis, Ramona, and Tom. Ray's half-brother also left a wife and three children living in Michigan.

Somehow Harold managed to tell Doug what happened to his uncle before they arrived at the airport. Ray and his family had been attending a birthday party for Greg Noble, their baby grandson. After enjoying a good visit, Ray had suggested a ride in his airplane.

In good spirits, Ray called the Nobles' dog to jump aboard, and then headed to Mount Horeb Airport with his half-brother, Eddie. He turned the plane west to land in Mineral Point where they refueled. Ray topped off the tank and then headed back up for a view of the town. He suffered a heart attack soon after takeoff.

Ray's death made Harold feel conscious of his responsibilities and very aware of his mortality. He quit smoking that fall, spurred on by Ray's death and his work on the farm.

Once he was aware that he should stop smoking, quitting happened fast. The cattle had gotten out when a rotten fence post gave way. Doug was at school and Walter was busy with the hogs, so Harold had to chase the herd back through the woods and up a hill by himself. He was puffing so hard by the time he reached the top of the hill that he had to double over. When he straightened up, he reached in his cigarette pocket, pulled out his "Wings," and threw them as far away as he could. He never smoked after that, but he did take up chewing tobacco like his father.

■ ■ ■

As the beef herd increased, the children became more and more important to the farming business. David had always warned against doing farm work after dark. "That's when farmers and their children lose fingers and even worse," he said. Harold hated to ask more of his children after a long day of school and chores.

However, children were expected to help on a farm, and they never complained when Harold ousted them from their beds at three o'clock in the morning to load cattle. The semis turned around in the yard and backed up to the cattle chute. They loaded cattle in the dark so that the trucks could be on their way by daylight. If they were lucky, the steers moved in an orderly fashion and did not escape between the chute and the doors of the truck.

The herd was almost two hundred and fifty head with both cows and bulls. During the summer when the pastures were lush, it was no problem to keep them fed. In the winter sometimes there were not enough hours in the day to haul feed for all the cattle, especially in a snow storm.

One year the temperature had been below zero for days, and Walter and Harold were trying to keep the pipes thawed to water the cattle. They had finished giving the animals half of what they really needed, when Walter discovered they had a cow in early labor.

The cow was old, but strong, and both men wanted to save her. She would get up, lie down, and get up again. When they put her in a pen to immobilize her and check her, it was apparent the calf needed turning. Walter was able to do that, but when the cow gave birth a little later, it was to a deformed calf, born dead.

Walter went back to work on the pipes. Harold, disturbed over the unfortunate birth, headed up the icy barnyard to the house. He could hear the cattle bawling as he went to get the children to help. It was late and dark. He was bone weary.

Then, wham! He hit a patch of ice and fell hard. He blacked out for a moment before he struggled up and limped painfully on into the kitchen. "Jeannie, Maggie, Doug, get down here and help me with the silage!" His voice was full of impatience and bitterness. His leg hurt like the very Devil. The next morning it was swollen and bruised.

Amy told him at breakfast, "It was eleven o'clock when you wakened the children to help feed." They still shoveled silage by hand back then, and Harold had been very stern with them.

"It's not an easy life," Harold agreed, rubbing his leg and hoping the weather would break soon.

■ ■ ■

Harold always told the children to ask Uncle Walter when they had problems with their homework. Even though he had suggested it, Harold was still surprised to realize that night after night Walter would sit down with his nieces and nephew to help them.

Like David, Walter had become a somewhat intimidating man in appearance, and certainly stern, but he was also a very good teacher and a kindly man. A stickler for punctuation and grammar, he saw to it that the children learned well. While they tended to their reading, writing, and figuring, he would pull out the latest copy of *The Scientific American*. He read it from cover to cover, sometimes getting out his notebook to jot down ideas.

One morning Harold had a bite to eat, and then bundled up, all set to go out and finish chores and take the children to school. In the winter the cows would come in the shed at night, so it needed to be mucked out before the kids could leave. The kitchen seemed cold despite the fire in the cookstove. Harold tried to scratch off the frost on the window so that he could see the thermometer. Just then Walter came in, shutting the door carefully behind him.

"Don't bother with the thermometer, Harold. It's too cold for man and beast. We've begun cleaning the shed, but we can't do a good job. I can't start the car, either. The battery is dead. It won't turn over in the cold."

"The children will welcome a day off," Harold volunteered.

"What about school?" Walter asked, looking just like their father did when his mind was made up.

Harold stared at him, and then headed out into the cold. The Thomas children never missed school because of the weather. Sometimes they would have to head out across the fields because the drifts were so high.

"Hurry up with the chores," Harold said, and directed his steps to the barn to hitch the horses to the bobsled. He spread the sleigh box with hay and blankets, and then he proceeded to build a hay house in the back where the children could cuddle up out of the wicked wind that persisted in its merciless howling.

Walter smiled slightly as the children settled into the bobsled. Harold signaled the horses and set out for town, praying that the horses could manage the drifts. At times like this he wondered if his father and Walter did not overestimate the value of an education.

Chapter 26

THE FOURTH GENERATION GROWS UP

Doug and his father, May 2007.
Photo by author.

On the farm the difficult years were balanced by the better ones, and for the children it was an ideal life. There was plenty for them to do, both work and play.

They all had a fascination for the railroad, Jeannie most of all. She cherished the experience she had one winter's day when there was a pounding on their door. Amy opened it to find a tall man in a long black duster. Jeannie, peeking from behind her mother, could not take her eyes off "the train person." He explained his visit as he stomped off the snow from his boots. "Excuse me, ma'am, our train is stuck in the snow out by the viaduct in your back pasture. I was hoping that I could use your phone and report the problem."

After the phone call, he directed his complete attention to Jeannie. He shook her hand. "What's your name, young lady?" he asked. "Perhaps you might like to take a ride on the train one day soon?"

"Oh, yes sir," she said, "that would be lovely."

The train man smiled and looked at Amy, "You just work that out with your mother. It's been a real pleasure meeting you."

In the summer Jeannie and her sisters and brother ran to the pasture where they would sit under the railroad bridge, thrilling to the sound of the whistle and enjoying all that weighty power rushing overhead, sparks a-flying, and the trestle shaking as if in an earthquake.

As the tracks grew older, the trains went much slower to avoid going off the tracks. One afternoon, Doug and his father headed up to that pasture to check on the cattle. The fences were a little loose, and they were missing one steer. Doug yelled, "Look up by the crossing." There was the steer, right on the tracks.

As Harold circled north to head the steer away from the tracks, he heard a whistle and looked up to see a diesel moving slowly around the bend. Harold motioned to the engineer, who slowed down even more when he saw the steer ambling along between the rails, taking his time.

Doug waved his arms like a wild man. "Dad, hey, Dad," he shouted, and Harold hopped on the train which was going very slowly toward the steer and the railroad bridge.

Then the steer moved a little toward the bridge.

Harold yelled. The train closed the gap.

The steer realized his legs were going through the spaces between the ties on the bridge. Suddenly, without a worry about the outcome, the steer jumped off the ties, over the rails and down onto the ground, where he took off like he had been shot. Harold waited until the train had crossed the bridge and then hopped off himself. Doug just shook his head in disbelief.

It was not much later in 1985 that the rails were torn up and the roadbed made into a bike path.

■ ■ ■

The railroad changed over the years, but getting in wood for the winter never did. The men had to go up in the woods, cut trees, trim them, and rough cut them. Then they carried the logs out of the woods to the manure spreader, which they used as a wagon to transport the logs to the house. There, they cut and split them into manageable chunks for burning in the wood stoves.

It is said that when you burn wood to heat in the winter, it warms you twice—once when you cut it, and the second time when you burn it. There was some truth to that, but not much humor. The Thomas family usually had to fit woodcutting into that miserable time of year after Indian summer and before the first big snow. There were just too many other things to do in the summer and fall.

After the fall farm work was done and the wood was cut, Amy and Harold turned to music. They had been playing with a number of different bands, but they played with Schmelcher's Hot Shots for the longest time. In the fall of 1971 Harold decided to form his own band. He called it Harry and the Country Sweethearts. Doug played backup guitar and a little rhythm. Amy sang and played the bass. Harold played lead fiddle, guitar, or whatever. His friends filled in when they could. He liked to practice at home and enjoyed having the kids hang around listening. It was a spirit-lifter for all of them, even if the pay was meager.

One winter Harold spent every night after dinner playing the guitar and scratching down chords. "Now listen, Amy, this one's for you to sing." She smiled and came over to see what he was doing. "We're going to Nashville," he said. She read over the words softly and they sang them together.

"I'll follow you to Nashville," she said, and they started to sing the song over from the beginning. Harold had aspirations of breaking into the country music scene. He wrote the lyrics as well as the music, and eventually sent some of his best songs to Nashville. He sent a tape recording too, but he never heard back.

He continued to write songs for Amy to sing:
"Heavenly Moments" come back to me, purer than gold
Shadows of the night fade away,
Just by the rays of the new coming day—

And he wrote some songs to sing to her:

I dreamed of our romance
Midst the wind and swirling sand
With rapture swelling high,
I whispered softly with a sigh,
You are my "Living Paradise."

Their audience seemed to enjoy his songs. Once the band warmed up a crowd, it played Harold's favorite lively tune making the dancers swing and sway as Amy sang:

When you're doing "The Jumping Walk,"
Sway, jump when you walk.
    Do it with that double talk,
    Don't forget to scratch and jive,
    Do it with a personal drive
    Be Bopping, like a fire fly, jumping jive.

The crowds liked one called "I Didn't Know" though Harold was not sure it was his best. It had sky/my rhymes and such, but folks liked the simple ballad. He used the steel guitar and sang it himself.

He was especially proud of "Spring." Sometimes the audience called for it even at Christmas and Valentine's dances. The lines went:

Oh, give me a spring and its companion
I live a life of sweet times
I will dream of the flowers and sunshine
I will stroll through the meadows and forests
I will speak delicate words and phrases
That make throbbing hearts ever sing
Illuminate every corner with light
Every cloud though be cast into the depths
    of eternal life.
Oh, give me a spring and its companion
And I will build a castle
And indeed live like a king.

■ ■ ■

Amy and Harold never said no to entertaining the veterans. One Friday night they headed north with Schmelcher's Hot Shots. They had been hired to play a hall that night and the next day they were to play at two veterans' homes. While she was singing, Amy was enjoying herself with a drink or two. She and Harold were singing a duet when she just fell off the stage as gracefully as you please. Someone called the EMTs while Harold persisted in trying to wake her up.

As the crowd parted to make way for a stretcher, Amy opened her eyes. The EMTs took her blood pressure and found that it was very, very low. They were all for taking her to the hospital, but Amy remembered they had a performance the next day at the veterans' hospital. After promising to go to the doctor on Monday, she persuaded the EMTs to leave, and Amy settled down with a cup of tea. They entertained the veterans the next day. Making music made them both forget personal problems and the difficulties of farming for profit.

Harold was involved with more than music and farming. By this time he had "completed all the chairs" in the Odd Fellows. The Fellows were quite impressed with his quick progress moving up the ranks, but it seemed no great accomplishment to Harold. It just took lots of memorizing, and he did that easily with music. It also took good works, such as visiting the sick and disabled, and Harold specialized in visiting the sick. These folks seemed to enjoy his jokes and sometimes he would sing them a song. It was another nice change from farm work.

■ ■ ■

The girls slipped away from the farm, one by one. Diana attended the University of Wisconsin and received her degree in Elementary Education. Her family was very proud of her achievements, but did not like to have her living so far away in Connecticut where she taught first grade.

Jeannie gave college a try and then she found a job in Madison and has been there ever since. Maggie was almost out of high school when she came to a dance where her parents were playing. There she met Lyle, and they have been together ever since.

After graduation from high school, Doug listened to Walter and went on to the vocational technical school for two years. He did exceptionally well at agricultural mechanics. There wasn't a tractor he could not tear apart or a car he could not fix.

It seemed that every night at the dinner table Doug had another idea about his future. Sometimes he was going into business with his cousin, Tom. They would buy a semi and travel cross-country together making lots of money. Often he talked about going on to special training for operating heavy equipment. "They pay upwards of twenty dollars an hour," he said. His family always listened to his ideas, but there never seemed a right time for him to leave. Walter had slowed down considerably, and Harold sure was glad to have Doug's help around the farm.

Chapter 27

LOSING GRANDMA AND WALTER

Lena collecting eggs.

The family all called Lena "Grandma," and she made her place in the family life as she had always done, by helping where she could and never interfering. In her home's familiar setting, blindness wasn't an obstacle. The little rocker by the stove in the kitchen remained her special place. She would sit and rock, sometimes to the beat of a good Swiss music radio station, sometimes singing along with familiar tunes and occasionally yodeling, to the children's great delight.

When Diana was in high school, she studied German so she could read the letters Grandma received from Switzerland, and then she would write the responses. Some of her translations were educated guesses because the Swiss dialect was not exactly schoolbook German, but that mattered little to either of them.

Lena's quiet strength and gentle humor enveloped them all. The grandchildren especially responded to her gentle teasing, and they enjoyed her childhood stories. She was still active around the farm. "Maggie," she would call, "please help me find my cane so I can go outside." The little girl marveled at her grandma's ability to navigate the barnyard and weed the flower garden.

Mavis, one of Margarette's oldest girls, visited the farm as often as possible and occasionally stayed the night with her grandma. Bedtime was a ritual of listening. The little girl read from the *Bible*, and then the two of them listened to the red-winged black birds settle down to sleep before they said their prayers and drifted off. In the morning Mavis brushed her grandma's hair until it shone like silver. After dressing, they headed for the hen house where Lena unfalteringly found each hen's nest and collected the eggs.

As a little boy, Doug was amazed at his grandma's strength. There was a playful competitiveness between the two of them. When he became cocky, she would challenge him. "You're such a strong little boy," she suggested, "try this," and she kept her knees straight and leaned over to touch the floor with the palms of her hands. He was tempted to test her ability to do things despite her blindness, but he was usually restrained either by his mother or his grandmother. As he grew older, Doug loved to go to Lena's room and talk.

Amy always accepted Lena's help with the dishes. Grandma also wanted to help with the cooking, canning, and freezing. Even towards the end, she continued to peel apples. It was a blessing for them all that Grandma Lena was never bedridden. In 1978, Lena suffered a sudden stroke. They took her to the hospital where she died. Lena had lived ninety-five years.

■ ■ ■

While his mother was alive, Harold felt confident and optimistic about farming. He believed the markets would turn around, the weather would improve, and the machinery would hold up. His thinking had nothing to do with logic. When Lena died, he saw things he did not want to see. He saw the leak in the barn roof, the antiquated milking equipment, the bull that was more a pet than a breeder, the baler that needed replacing, and the loans that never seemed to be paid up.

Their old New Holland 77 baler tells the story. Of course the baler worked well when it was new, but they had used it hard in the sixties and seventies. Eventually they struggled to bale three loads a day. The baler had a problem tying, leaving more and more broken bales. Before the baler finally gave out, they were lucky if they made one load a day, and what they really needed was three *cuttings* of hay to carry the cattle over the winter.

At first the men never questioned their ability to find parts and fix the baler. There were many old New Holland 77's around— in their neighbor's fields, in the old rock quarry in Dodgeville, and in the junk yard in Mineral Point. Mainly they were looking for needles to replace the bent and broken ones that tied the bales, but eventually they had to go farther and farther away to find replacement parts, and finally they ran out of places to go.

They called shops to have the needles welded, but the welders never fixed them quite right, and they had more broken bales. The year Lena died, Walter was still cutting the first crop hay when it started to snow. It took them all summer, because they were having so much trouble with the baler.

■ ■ ■

For awhile now, Amy had been working at nearby Stauffer's cheese factory. She had suggested it. "I would really like doing something different," she said. Harold told her that she could use the money she made for whatever she wanted. When Reiser's in Mount Horeb offered more money for their night shift, she worked for them, sometimes as a supervisor and sometimes as ordinary labor. Harold would drive Amy over to Mount Horeb and pick her up every day. She had told him, "If I go to work, I'll buy a silo unloader."

Harold and Walter never paid much mind to her working until she plunked fifteen hundred dollars down on the kitchen table and announced, "Here's the money. Buy a silo unloader." She never did like to unload silage by hand. She also bought a good used car and then she bought a throw baler for seven hundred and fifty dollars. It is the same baler they are using today. It works well. Harold never did hear what Amy bought for herself.

By the time Lena died, Walter was able to do less and less on the farm. He was quieter and slower, focusing all his strength and attention on his pigs.

Walter had always been strict. In fact, the children believed he was a little over-controlling. Later they might admit he was right most of the time, old-fashioned in some ways, but right. Walter also had a subtle sense of humor and a neat turn of words that surprised them and made them think and often chuckle. However, in the last few years he spoke little, and when he did, the words were often heavy with bitterness and even sarcasm.

Walter had become the lawyer for his generation, and he would not back down to anyone. Usually it was just hunters who thought nothing of trespassing the land during deer and turkey season, but he really showed his mettle when he came up against the Department of Transportation. The Thomas cattle were pastured on both sides of the highway. They used an underpass to get across. The DOT intended to widen Highway 18/151 by two lanes. They planned to give the Thomases a six-foot underpass.

Walter actually held up construction until the Department of Transportation agreed to give them an eight-foot underpass for their cattle.

Finally, Walter's doctor made it clear to him that he was suffering from congestive heart failure. He needed an operation. Open-heart surgery sounded like a challenge that he would have to take on. It was getting increasingly difficult for Walter to do anything worthwhile on the farm.

Margarette came to the farm to see him off the morning Harold and Amy drove him to Madison. Walter gripped her hand as he leaned toward her and said gruffly, "Take care of the barn."

Doug had taken him for one last ride around the farm the day before. He might have guessed that his uncle was not coming back.

Walter was not alone on the day of the surgery. His brother and sister and all his nieces and nephews were with him to wish him well.

When it came Evelyn's turn to have a private word with her uncle, he pulled her close and apologized for selling the old horses and not telling her.

Walter never came home from the hospital.

■ ■ ■

After Walter's death in 1987, Harold sold all the pigs. "I never did like pigs," Doug recalled. "They are too ornery, especially the sows when they have piglets, always "coming in" during the night. "Ah, that was a horrible job," he concluded.

Pigs were often called "mortgage-lifters" because they were said to be a quick financial turnaround, but it never seemed to work that way for the Thomas family. They rarely had enough feed for the pigs as well as the beef cows, so they had to buy feed, thus losing their profit. Walter had kept pigs even though they lost money season after season.

By 1999, the Thomas farm operation was a lot simpler with power silage feeders. Harold rented bulls to settle their cow herd, and they raised calves to sell as steers. By the turn of the century, they had seventeen cows and fifteen calves.

The Thomases had stayed close to the farm for many years. Occasionally, Harold wondered what another life would be like. He reread a poem of his father's written years ago, and even toyed with the thought of setting it to music:

I stopped upon the highway,
　and looked the country round.
I saw the gold tinged forests,
　and the cornfields turning brown.
I saw geese winging southward.
　I saw cattle huddled in the draw.
And, I saw the kicking colts,
　alarmed at my flapping mackinaw.
I trudged a little further,
　and then I paused and stopped.
I arrived at this conclusion.
　stay here or I must not.
Vagabond I am, yet that is I,
　I follow all summer's friends.
I sense the coming winter,
　so farewell you barren land.
I'm off to good old Mexico
　or maybe Southern Spain,
And if I like the balmy clime,
　well sure, I'll be back again.

Chapter 28

ESTABLISHING
A LEGACY

Harold Thomas.

As the end of the century drew nearer, Harold became increasingly aware that the stone barn needed repair. The roof continued to leak and an occasional stone fell out of its appointed place. The farm operation kept them going, but there was little extra money for fixing things up.

For many years Doug had been working full time in Dodgeville at Lands' End, and Amy was retired from the cheese factory. Harold worked on the farm and depended on Doug's help when he was free.

"Amy, Doug, look at this," Harold said as he spread out an article on farms that had been in one family for over a century. At the bottom of the page was an application for a "Century Farm."

"You're reaching for straws, Dad. They're not going to be giving us any money to repair the barn," Doug answered after a quick look.

"I don't have time for that kind of thing," Amy said, getting back to her bread baking.

But Harold did have time, and he believed it just might get them the recognition they deserved for preserving the farm and the stone barn for so long.

The application was simple and straightforward. The state wanted proof of one hundred years of continuous family ownership. Ol' Watt, David, Walter, and Harold David Thomas. One hundred years of Thomas ownership in three generations, and Doug would make it four. The most difficult part was writing a "short narrative about significant events of the farm's history up to its current operations." Harold found a good photo of the stone barn and included it with the application which he sent in long before the deadline of January 15th.

Not too long after the end of January he received an impressive certificate noting their achievement—they had been named a "Century Farm." He marked the calendar for the special program at the Wisconsin State Fair, but never took time to attend. However, Harold continued to reach out after this achievement. While he did not realize it at the time, it really was a new beginning.

■ ■ ■

Over the years many visitors came and went, and each one of them said how astonishing the stone barn was. One man drove in from Washington state. Another man and his wife with Florida license plates stopped by. Like most visitors, they took a picture of Harold in front of the stone barn door. A Channel 21 reporter stayed for over two hours photographing the farm and barn and Harold for a special called "Wisconsin Stories" which aired on national television.

Some architects from the University of Wisconsin said that the stone barn would cost between five hundred thousand and one million dollars to build. "I do believe there are two, no three different kinds of arches used in this building," one architect claimed excitedly.

Another architect pointed out the large doors on the north, west, and east elevations. "They're called 'basket-handle arches.' Just see how the keystones protrude from the wall plane slightly." Then he pointed to the ventilators. "We call those half-round or Roman arches. They are supported from the interior with those large wood timber lintels."

The architects explained to Harold, "Just look very carefully at the arches and you will find virtually no mortar between the joints of those wedge shaped arch stones called *voussoirs*. Fine craftsmanship is what enables a mason to use very little mortar to form the arches."

Harold nodded and smiled at their knowledge and enthusiasm about the treasure he knew so well.

The architects used technical terms for the barn and admired it very much, but still they drove away without really coming up with a solution to help preserve it.

■ ■ ■

Derek Johnson was different. Not only did he admire the stone barn, but he had identified something special about the Thomas land. He was a director of the internationally recognized Nature Conservancy. The motto of this organization is "saving the last great places on earth." The Nature people believed that the Thomas pasture was a "great place."

Doug was incredulous. "The cattle think it's great, but right now it's a bit overgrown with weeds." It turned out that those "weeds" were just the reason The Nature Conservancy was so interested in the property. The "weeds" were marbleseed, Hill's thistle, wooly milkweed, and tuberous Indian plantain. They were common in the original prairie that once covered the Midwest. Furthermore, they contributed to the habitat of the endangered *Regal Fritillary* butterfly.

Derek continued to explain, "Some special bird species nest in your back pasture—the upland sandpiper, vesper sparrow, and western meadowlark." He said The Nature Conservancy wanted to buy the eighty-acre pasture, and they wanted to keep it as a prairie forever.

Amy and Doug could tell that Harold was excited about the purchase price. The three of them realized that Walter might never have talked to the Johnson fellow, but perhaps Walter might have considered the proposition had he realized that the eighty acres would stay the same forever. It would never be developed into a subdivision full of outsized homes.

"We just might have to cut down on our beef herd," Doug said.

Amy nodded with little regret.

Harold sold the back pasture to The Nature Conservancy in 1997. His nephew Tom Osborn printed off what was said about their land on The Nature Conservancy Website. The heading read, "Barneveld Prairie, a Remnant of a Once-Widespread Habitat." The description followed:

> *This is a great place to see a remnant of the*
> *vast tall grass prairies and savannas that*
> *once covered most of southern Wisconsin.*
> *Surrounded by an agricultural landscape,*
> *the hilltops and valleys at Barneveld Prairie*
> *provide habitat for colorful butterflies*
> *and uncommon birds that thrive in large,*
> *open, treeless landscapes.*

■ ■ ■

Visitors continued to stop by the farm. One group called Cameraworks was especially enjoyable. There were almost a dozen semi-professional photographers in this group. Loaded with fancy equipment, even lights to use inside the barn, they spent an entire morning listening to Harold tell stories and taking photos from all angles.

About a month later, the man who had carried the most camera equipment stopped by with a framed enlargement of the inside of the barn showing how remarkable it looked with the light streaming into the interior through the louvers and the open door. Amy hung the photo in their front room.

Among the photographers was a lady named Anne Bachner who had visited the farm before and had talked to Harold about the National Register of Historic Places. She loved old barns and believed that the best should be preserved. She thought getting the Thomas Stone Barn on the register just might help.

At first Harold failed to see any point of having the barn on a register. There was no money given for this achievement, and what they needed was money to repair the roof, not their name on another list.

At this same time, a young man named David Lowe occasionally dropped by. He was an archeologist who had found many Native American rock art sites in Iowa County and had succeeded in placing those sites on the Register for Historic Places. He was fascinated with the stone barn as well as the prairie and agreed that getting the barn on the National Register would be helpful.

Anne Bachner and David Lowe, with Harold's permission, decided to team up on the project. It seemed like it took them a long time to do the measurements and take the required photos, but Harold realized they did have other things on their minds besides the stone barn. Meanwhile, in 1999 John Oncken published a feature article on the stone barn in *The Capital Times* entitled, "Will modern technology build anything (as) enduring?"

Finally, in March of 2001 the Thomas Stone Barn was placed on both the State and National Register of Historic Places. Susan Lampert Smith from *The Wisconsin State Journal* came to interview the family and take photos.

While Walter might have walked away from these conservancy folks because he never believed outsiders could save the stone barn, Harold felt he was doing the right thing by placing it on the Register. He learned later that it was easier to take the next step in saving and repairing the barn since the Register "experts in the field of architecture and history" saw the stone barn with the same eyes as the Thomases did, as a very important and exceptional structure.

■ ■ ■

Farm life continued uneventfully with its seasonal challenges and pleasures until Harold met Doug Cieslak in 2003. Doug Cieslak was the director of the Driftless Area Land Conservancy, headquartered in Dodgeville, Wisconsin. Doug admired the barn, but he seemed more interested in the farm land. "The Conservancy," he explained, "wants to preserve rural open spaces and natural areas."

"Well," Harold paused, "we want to preserve the farm land, but we want to save the barn too, and we want to continue farming."

Doug Cieslak looked hard at Harold. "Why don't you show me the barn," he said. Harold showed him the mow half full of hay and explained the hay chutes, the old hay rail, the ventilators, the arches, and the date stone. He told some stories about Ol' Watt, David and his brothers. Doug Cieslak did not want Harold to stop talking, but the afternoon was getting away from them. Mr. Cieslak was overwhelmed. "This barn must be saved," he nodded. "It must be preserved."

"Come anytime," Harold said as Doug climbed into his truck. Harold joined Amy and his son Doug for dinner. The family chuckled about Mr. Cieslak's enthusiasm, thinking he was just another person who loved their land and their barn, but who really could not help. They believed that they would probably never see him again. They were wrong on both counts.

Luckily, Doug Cieslak, executive director of a fledgling land conservancy organization, believed that he could put his words into action. He visited the Thomases again and presented his idea. "Perhaps we can put an easement on your farm land that would protect it from being developed, and preserve and restore the barn at the same time."

"It sounds too good to be true," Harold offered.

Doug Cieslak explained that the Thomases could sell the Conservancy a conservation easement on the farm. Then Harold could use the proceeds of the sale to repair the barn. It was a difficult idea for the Thomas family to understand at first. The Driftless Area Land Conservancy would pay them money to repair the barn and keep it repaired, forever? And the Conservancy would see that the farm was never overrun with housing developments? And the Thomases would still own the farm?

After talking to so many folks who admired the barn and wanted to preserve it but did nothing, they had finally met someone who claimed to be really able to help them. Doug Cieslak was the Conservancy spokesperson, but the Thomases met others from the organization who made them feel confident that the group could indeed do what it promised. The closing date for the transaction was March 10, 2005.

Harold and his son Doug arrived at the office before the lawyers on that momentous day. The signing went smoothly, and Doug Cieslak expressed his appreciation for the generous conditions that Harold offered in the agreement. The property would remain a farm forever. It would never be developed. Finally, the old stone barn could get a new roof, maybe by fall, using the proceeds of the easement sale.

There was to be a celebration. It was not just for the Thomas family and their neighbors. It was not just for the Driftless Area Land Conservancy. The invitation list included over one thousand names from the Governor to leaders in The Nature Conservancy, the Department of Natural Resources, the Friends of Military Ridge Trail, The Prairie Enthusiasts, the local historical societies and many others.

The Wisconsin State Journal printed a compelling article the Saturday before the event. It told that the celebration was free, and that folks could tour the barn, enjoy refreshments, listen to some old-time music and hear a man named Jerry Apps speak on farming. Apps was a famous rural author who had written many great Wisconsin books on barns, cheese factories, and farming.

Sunday, April 24th, 2005, dawned brilliantly cool and very windy. The sun had just enough warmth to make folks think spring could well be coming. Winter had been long, and they needed some good excuse to get outside. The Thomas Stone Barn Event proved to be a wonderful diversion.

For Harold and his extended family and for the Driftless Area Land Conservancy, the day began quietly with each person helping set up for the day. Some folks moved hay bales to create a stage area in the barn for the speaker, others set up displays for a variety of conservation organizations in the machine shed, and some set out the refreshments and arranged potted plants.

A mounted unit of the local Knights of Columbus unloaded their horses, saddled up, and began guiding the cars into the hay field which Harold and Doug planned for parking. It was well before the scheduled time for the opening, but people began drifting in. They found Folklore Village musicians in the barn playing old-time favorites on acoustic instruments.

Anne Bachner, the lady who loved barns, the archeologist/prairie enthusiast, David Lowe, and an expert in laying up stone named Roland Sardeson explained the Thomas legacy again and again to crowds that soon became almost overwhelming. The newspapers estimated over seven hundred folks attended.

All the cookies were eaten in the first hour or so. The drinks were consumed soon after. The barn was packed with folks listening to the music and the speakers. They were respectfully quiet as Harold walked slowly up to the improvised stage. He anticipated sharing his heritage with everyone.

Harold looked out over the crowd of folks in his barn. They were waiting for him to speak. The familiar hay mow was packed with people he could see only in a blur of unnaturally brilliant light. He knew they wanted to hear the stories that were in his heart and in the hearts of his family.

He looked up to the rafters. They wanted to see Margarette as he could, swinging hand-over-hand along the hay rail. And they wanted to see Great-grandma carrying three buckets of water up from the well and Lena sitting in her little white rocker in the kitchen and Amy telling stories to the children.

They wanted to learn about Ol' Watt, the visionary who dared to dream of a barn that was as majestic as a cathedral and as strong as a fortress. Harold looked at his friends on the stage who introduced him so kindly and who had done so much to save the barn. He could see in their faces that they really were interested in David and the sacrifices he made to keep the barn and farm in the family. They were interested in him, as well, and his son's ideas for the future of the farm and stone barn.

Harold searched his pockets for his notebook and took it out, then looked again at the bright mass of faces. Harold acknowledged the folks, welcomed their interest, but ultimately said little and told no stories. He smiled apologetically. There was too much to tell in one short afternoon. He had help saving the barn and the farm, perhaps he would find help telling the stories.

Walter could have defined the mystery of the arches, but may well have turned away from the crowd as Harold did. David, who could have spoken on anything, probably would not have explained what he gave up for the family farm. Ol' Watt might have outlined the economics of feeding out cattle during the winter, but could never have verbalized what the stone barn really meant to him. Fortunately for all, because of the Thomas legacy, the stone barn itself was speaking and would continue to speak, most eloquently, for itself.

The End

Thomas Stone barn with Blue Mounds as background and a field of soybeans in the foreground. Photo by Doug Cieslak.

BIBLIOGRAPHY

Hay fork used in the stone barn.

Apps, Jerry. *Barns of Wisconsin.* Madison: Wisconsin Trails, 1997.

Barney, Maginel Wright. *The Valley of the God-Almighty Joneses.* Spring Green: Unity Chapel Publications, 1986.

Berg, Donald J. *American Country Building Design,* New York: Sterling Publication Co., 1997.

Boyer, Dennis. *Iowa County Folktales.* Dodgeville: Eagletree Press, 1994.

Curtis, John T. *The Vegetation of Wisconsin, an Ordination of Plant Communities.* Madison: The University of Wisconsin Press, nd.

Derleth, August. *Wisconsin Country, A Sac Prairie Journal.* New York: The Candlelight Press, 1965.

Helmenstine, John F. *Weehaukaja, a History of the Village of Barneveld and the Town of Brigham* volumes 1. np, 1976.

Helmenstine, John F. *Weehaukaja, a History of the Village of Barneveld and the Town of Brigham,* volume 2. np, 1977.

History of Iowa County, Wisconsin. Chicago, Iowa County Bicentennial Education Committee, 1881.

Isthmus Architecture, Inc. *Thomas Stone barn, Historic Structure Report.* np/nd.

Leopold, Aldo. *A Sand County Almanac and Sketches Here and There.* New York: Oxford University Press, 1949.

McDaniel, David P. "Spring City and the Water War of 1892." *Wisconsin Magazine of History,* Autumn 2005.

McRaven, Charles. *Building With Stone.* Pownal, Vermont, Story Communications, Inc., 1989.

Margaret Metcalf and Violet Williams and Marion Pustina. *Schools of Iowa County.* Blanchardville: Ski Printers, September 1976.

Palliser, George and Charles, *Palliser's Model Homes.* Bridgeport, Conn. 1878.

Phillips, Melva. *A Look to the North of Military Ridge.* np/nd.

Sloane, Eric. *An Age of Barns.* New York: Funk & Wagnalls Publishing Company, Inc., 1967.

Smith, William Rudolph. *Incidents of a Journey From Pennsylvania to Wisconsin Territory, in 1837.* Chicago: Wright Howes, 1927.

Thesz, Lou with Kit Bauman. *"Hooker: An Authentic Wrestler's Adventures Inside the bizarre World of Pro Wrestling."* np/nd .

INTERVIEWS, EMAILS, TAPES, DOCUMENTS AND MEMORABILIA

Margarette at age 22.

Buck, Sadie (Sarah). *Letter* from Pueblo, Colorado, to Lottie Thomas. December 11, 1894.

Buck, Sadie (Sarah). *Letter* from Pueblo, Colorado to Walter Thomas. June 18th, 1898.

Downs, David. *Phone interview* about Walter's hole in the heart. January 4th, 2005.

Indenture for Nant Y. Willen Cheese factory, 1891.

McClosky, James. *Letter* from Burke, Idaho, to Walter Thomas. December 13, 1894.

McClosky, James. *Letter* from Burke, Idaho, to Walter "Ol' Watt" Thomas, January 1, 1895.

Oncken, John. "Will modern technology build anything enduring?" *The Capital Times*. Madison, 1995.

Osborn, Margarette Thomas. *Biography* of her father, David D. Thomas written for a senior literature class, March 11, 1937.

Osborn, Margarette. *Phone interview*. October 2004.

Osborn, Tom. *Phone interview*. February 18, 2005.

Osborn, Tom. *e-mail*. April 18, 2005.

Petro, Diana. Saturday, *e-mail* about her life on the farm. January 15, 2005.

Recording Book for School District Number Nine of the Town of Ridgeway, County of Iowa, State of Wisconsin, North America, 1861 to October 27th, 1898.

Sorensen, Sterling. "1,300 At Community Picnic and Get-Together Held on Blue Mounds." *The Capital Times*. August 11, 1952.

Thomas, Arthur. *Letter* from Chicago, Illinois, to David Thomas. June 21, 1912.

Thomas, Arthur. *Letter* from Chicago, Illinois, to David Thomas. May 29, 1912.

Thomas, David Darius. *Fourth of July Oration*, 1894.

Thomas, David Darius. "Unfurl The Stars and Stripes" *a poem*.

Thomas, Harold. *Interview*. October, 2004.

Thomas, Harold, Maggie, Amy. *Interview*. March 12, 2005.

Thomas, Harold. *Phone interview* on dogs, church, century farms January 31, 2005.

Thomas, Harold. *Tape* including 5 original songs and one poem.